John Gross is a man of prayer and simplicity. I love his heart for the poor of the earth. This book is a must read for those who want to be touched by Gods heart for the nations. Come break-out of the mundane as ordinary Christian's, say yes to the call of Jesus and experience the rivers of living water as they find thirsty ground.

Mike Bickle, Director, International House of Prayer of Kansas City, MO

John is a man exemplary in godly character, who passionately loves Jesus and missions. His book is brilliantly simple and profoundly real while providing a healthy kingdom perspective of short-term missions and what it means to go as a disciple of Jesus to another nation.

Dr. John Wesley Adams, Associate Director
Fusion Ministries, Kansas City, MO

Where would God call you to let the river flow? If you are a seriously mission minded believer, read this book with an open heart and be challenged to be an agent of change by letting "The River Flow Down" through you.

Don Richter, Director
Harvest Preparation International Ministries Sarasota, FL

I highly recommend this book. It's filled with testimony to the supernatural power of God manifested through ordinary men and women and will pull at your heart to take the gospel to the poor, the broken, the lame, the orphan, the widow and the ones bound by Satan throughout the world."

Regina Shank, Apostolic Leader
Missouri Prayer Global Mission, Carthage, MO

John Gross

THE RIVER FLOWS DOWN

A Call to Missions for Ordinary Christians

PUBLISHED BY AMBASSADORS PRESS
AN EXTENSION OF AMBASSADORS INTERNATIONAL
PO Box 2187, Newburgh, N.Y. 64134
PO Box 9843, Kansas City, MO 64134

Printed in the United States of America

For further information and distribution, contact Publisher
AMBASSADORS PRESS, *northeastgatewaytofreedom@verizon.net;*
www.Ambassadors-International.com

First printing August 2006
Second printing February 2009

Developer - David Huff
Editor - Jackie Macgirvin
Cover Design - Paul Slaninka
Layout Artist - Dale Jimmo

Library of Congress Catalog Card Number: 2006930690
International Standard Book Number 978-0-9675552-4-9

TABLE OF CONTENTS

ACKNOWLEDGEMENTS

I would like to express my deepest thanks to my wife Dianna and to my family for extending grace and understanding as I continue to walk out this amazing journey.

For all those who gave time, talent and finances to make our trips possible, you have no idea the value you hold in my heart and in the hearts of those you touched in Uganda.

Liz Ray, and Mikki Olson, your crash course in English grammar helped this country boy immensely. Thanks to David Huff and Jackie Macgirvin, who spent hours, making my experiences into an orderly, readable book.

Thank you to the publisher of this book Ambassadors Press. Rosey Andrews, you saw the importance in this project as you have with so many others. David Huff, you opened a door for me that I didn't know was there by asking the right questions. I thought I was finished writing but you and Rosey helped me to see that I had just begun.

Thank you, Jesus for not leaving me comfortless, but sending Your Holy Spirit to be my present help in time of need.

John Gross
Kansas City, Missouri, USA

INTRODUCTION

"I can't." "I don't." "He can." "He does." I quickly learned my inability and His ability while on the mission field. My goal in writing this book is to offer a fresh look at missions from the ordinary person's perspective. God can and does use ordinary people.

What I discovered when I got to Africa was that I couldn't fix everything, and I couldn't make it all better. I wish it were as simple as when our children were young and a skinned knee could be fixed with a kiss. I don't have the answers to the hard questions that revolved around some of the sobering things I saw while I was there.

I do know who has the answers and the ability to do something lasting about these seemingly insurmountable problems—Jesus. That is not just a trite cliché. It's something I found was really true. Many times I felt closest to Him, as I was closest to those in need. Just being in touch with people in pain, just being there, just listening, just understanding, and just letting God be God gave me strength.

I often hear Americans say, "Why do you have to go halfway around the world when there are people in need right here?" While there are people in need everywhere we must know it is not need that compels us to go, but the voice of the Lord. Where He leads we must follow, whether next-door, down the street or around the world. An open ear and a willing heart are soft clay in the hand of the Potter. Oh how the Lord longs for soft clay.

While in Uganda I was asked to write a book about the message that God had put in my heart. Of course I laughed. I can't write and I surely can't spell, but something deep within me whispered, "You'll never know if you don't try."

My experience is hard to explain but I've come up with a name for it. I call it "spiritual gravity." That seems to be the best description of what you will find in these pages. My simple definition of spiritual gravity is "God lets His love flow down to us, we receive it and let it continue to flow through us out to all those who, just like us, are in need." It's like a mighty river flowing down into a valley, flowing from the melting snow as the bright spring afternoon has its way with winter's remains.

I don't have a college degree, just a Ph.D. from the school of hard knocks. I am a simple man who loves God, my wife, and the adventures of life. My prayer is that this little book challenges you to believe, God can use you the way He surely used me.

All you have to do is make yourself available and let *The River Flow Down!*

SIMON PETER—During worship at the Busia outreach Charles Jr. and I noticed a young boy looking at us through an air hole in the wall. He asked us to pray for him because he was sick. We stuck our hands through the wall and prayed for him. Later we found out his name was Simon Peter.

PART I

CHAPTER 1

The Beginning

We were somewhere over northern Africa when I looked out the plane's window and saw the sun starting to set. What I felt was beyond words, the pastel colors of the sunset would have made a great cover for National Geographic. My feeling was more than just the result of the beauty coupled with being on the opposite side of the world. It was this-- I was completely out of control for the first time in my life--nothing I could do would change anything, not even the direction I was heading. I realized I was in the center of the Lord's hand and will and all I could do was rest in awe of Him. So I did. Soon what little light was left was chased away by the darkness. Before long we were flying over Entebbe, Uganda. I could make out a few lights down below marking the runway.

Once we touched down I was chomping at the bit to get off the plane. However, when I saw armed guards with automatic weapons at the entry point of the airport a wave of apprehension slightly dampened my excitement. The portable stairs were maneuvered into place and our little team made the descent to African ground and headed toward the checkpoint.

Our team, the Charles family [Shawn, Laura and Kyle], my friend Kato and I presented our passports. Once through the gate, the guards checked our luggage and we moved out into the still warm Ugandan night air where we were greeted by our gracious hosts. Kato appeared to be something of a celebrity judging by the turnout of his friends and family at the airport in Entebbe.

After 30 hours of travel we were grateful to arrive at the Namirembe Guest House in Kampala. It was run by the Anglican Church of Uganda and provided a great place to use as our hub. By the time we got settled into bed and pulled our mosquito nets around us it was early morning May 21, 2001. We spent some time in prayer and one by one drifted off to sleep.

Who could have known that I, a small town pastor's son, who at one time was so far from God, would actually end up here on a short-term mission's trip? Only God.

MY REBELLIOUS YEARS

They say preacher's kids are the worst, and I didn't waste any time trying to change public opinion. By the time I was 18 I was as wild as fire, with a war raging in my belly. I married and nine days later my son, John David Jr. was born. By 20 I was so far gone only a mother could love me. Thank God my parents and Dianna, the greatest wife in the world, didn't give up on me. They kept praying and in just a little over three years time God answered them--loud and clear I might add -- but that three year wait was hard on everyone.

For example, on Dianna's 20th birthday I had been out partying all night. She was waiting up when I arrived home. She asked if I had thought to buy her a birthday card. In anger I emptied my pockets, threw the money at her, and spat, "Here, go buy your own *#%*& card." Looking back, I feel sick to think what I had become and what I put Dianna through. I never physically abused her, but living with me was an emotional nightmare.

Three years after John David was born Dianna became pregnant with Angela, our second child. At the hospital she pleaded, "John if you will come into the delivery room with me, I will never ask you to do another thing." I had not told her I was leaving, but somehow she knew. I was bent on self-destruction, while she was bent becoming a godly woman.

At the hospital, I thought to myself, *I'll go in the delivery room, then I am out of here.* What happened next saved my life, not to mention my soul. I heard the sound of an infant cry, and then the doctor said, "Here you go, Dad. Here's your new daughter." As I looked at Angela, I heard the clearest voice I had heard in years, but it wasn't from anyone in the room. The Lord thundered, "It's the end of the line." This was the beginning of getting back to God. No one would have guessed, but I had known God as a child.

MY LIFE AS A PK

My first memories of knowing God are around the age of five. My father was pastor of a small Southern Baptist church in Clarksburg, Missouri. Many nights he would go to church, lie on the floor and cry out for the Lord to visit him in power. Dad had read the book *The Cross and The Switchblade* by David Wilkerson, and hungered to see the power of God released in his life for evangelism. God began to breathe on a teen outreach center across the street from the church. Dad became a good friend of many a wild teenager.

One night he took me along on his Holy Spirit-seeking mission. He left me in his office to play on his typewriter while he prayed. I was clacking away on the keys having a good time, when I had the feeling someone was watching me. Behind me was a large painting of Jesus hanging on the cross. Though I had seen it many times before I was captured by it. It seemed to get bigger until it was all that I could see. I could feel the pain in Jesus' eyes, as He hung on the cross. Tears ran like rivers down my cheeks as the painting came alive. With a mixture of great pain and great love Jesus' eyes looked right through me. With great effort he pushed himself up to get a breath. His eyes fell on me again, and without words I knew that I knew He was suffering for me. Of course I knew about Jesus. I had been in church more than all my little friends and heard daily Bible stories but this was different than any story.

I bolted out of the room and found my father praying. "Dad," I exclaimed, "that man on the cross loves me!" Dad had me slow down and retell the experience. After he concluded my experience was genuine he was filled with great joy and he rushed me home to tell Mom so I could respond to Christ in a family setting. You see my parents didn't just pray at church, in our house the bed was the family altar and it was a very familiar place of prayer. That night I went to sleep knowing that I was a sinner who needed saving and that Jesus had provided that for me.

I loved God very much, but found the church to be somewhat of a contradiction to godliness. I tried to be a good Christian but at age 12 I starting living a secret life as I saw so many others do. I saw the "Doctor Jekyll and Mr. Hyde" style of Christianity practiced by many Christian adults, and frankly I was tired of the jokes at school about the hypocrites at church.

My Christian world came crashing down as I heard the news that a highly respected man in our church was leaving his wife and family to marry a teenager he had gotten pregnant. Also, I saw the pain inflicted from backbiting and gossip. Those two issues warred against my walk with God. The third problem was that I liked sin and found it was fun. At 16-years-old I was done with church and done with God--no more games, no more pretending.

By the time I was 21 my life seemed hopeless. The Apostle Paul said he was the chief of sinners, but that was only because I hadn't been born yet.

God knew that I was about to go to the point of no return. On March 5, 1982, God got my attention in that delivery room and turned me back from a life of hard-core sin. God had arrested me and given me the right to remain silent. I took it. It felt like every hellfire and brimstone message I had ever heard was sounding again in my ears. Those words I heard in the delivery room brought conviction, something I had not felt in a long, long time. The next thing I remember I was flushing all my alcohol and drugs down the toilet.

Eventually I returned to the church. Right away I noticed something that was different. I remember when I was growing up in the church every visiting missionary gave a presentation and an altar call for potential missionaries. I don't remember any of those services that someone wasn't called or at least thought he or she was.

However, when I returned to the church I found a different message. "God hasn't called you, but He has called me. You can sow into this hot soil and share in my reward of seeing souls saved." I wanted to stand up and yell, "How do you know I'm not called?"

In mid-2000 Dianna and I starting attending a home group led by Shawn and Laura Charles. There we met Kato. We didn't realize then that through knowing Kato we would end up on several short-term mission trips.

Kato was from Uganda and he challenged us by telling stories of the fields there that were white unto harvest. Kato hadn't seen his family in quite some time so we began to raise support to send him home for a visit.

CHAPTER 2

Kato's Testimony

I was born in Entebbe, Uganda, where my parents lived and worked. My father had been a pilot for the Ugandan government. In the early 1970's, when I was only eight-years-old, during the time of the notorious dictator Idi Amin, my parents fled for their lives to neighboring Kenya. We spent the next eight years exiled as refugees. We returned after Idi Amin's regime of terror was overthrown.

I was blessed that my parents gave all they had to get me educated. Children in Africa can only dream of a free education. I attended schools that were built by Anglican and Catholic missionaries. However, I did not have a personal relationship with the Lord.

SALVATION

I had watched African Evangelist Pastor Kayanja's broadcast on television, but stubbornly refused to surrender my life even though I felt very heavy conviction. I argued with what I then called "a voice." I said to this "voice" that I would only get saved if the preacher I saw on television came to our town. Surprisingly within days, I heard that he was holding a healing meeting here. I was amazed and shocked that God had heard my request. I went to the evangelistic healing meeting and could not wait for the pastor to call for those who wanted to get saved. I gave my life to Jesus Christ on September 16, 1989 and I have never looked back.

A number of my friends like Jackson Wadanya and Jimmy Kigwana, who are co-workers in the Lord's work in Uganda, got saved in the same meeting. Jackson is a now a statistician for the Ugandan government and has used his personal income to build and open the first brick church building in Busia, his home village.

Jimmy opened a church in Kajjansi. He also leads a Bible college where many local pastors find training.

I joined a local church in Entebbe for discipleship and growth in the Lord's Word. Together with my friends we studied the Bible, prayed and formed a weekly hospital outreach ministry. We shared Jesus with the hurting souls in the hospitals and prayed for healing. At times we would return the next week and those we had prayed for would be getting discharged because they were healed. The Lord was faithful and He did just that to the amazement of the doctors.

During that time I was still in high school. I got involved with school evangelism. We preached the gospel from class to class and witnessed to the teachers too. I spoke to almost every student in my school about Jesus, but no one gave his or her life to Christ. I didn't realize at that time that I was sowing seeds. The harvest came later when my former schoolmates gave their lives to Jesus Christ.

During school breaks I went to villages with my church's team. It was at this time that I met Pastor Paul Busulwa who came to our high school to do a follow up on all who had given their lives to Jesus at the evangelistic meeting. For a year Paul taught us how to pray, study the Bible and witness to other students. He laid a firm foundation for us in Christ Jesus.

After high school I decided I was going to dedicate a number of years in service to Jesus before I entered college. I got involved in a number of prayer movements in Entebbe and grew in intercession, spending much time studying God's Word with prayer and fasting. I had the opportunity to work as a youth pastor at the Entebbe Power Christian Center. I also led praise and worship in the church. This propelled me into a deeper love for Jesus. I traveled extensively with

Paul, Jimmy and the pastoral team at the Power Christian Center, visiting village after village, preaching the gospel and praying for the sick.

God was always faithful to honor His Word through healings, miracles, and by delivering people from the Devil's oppression. I witnessed many that were delivered from all kinds of demonic oppressions. For 10 years I was blessed to watch the Lord saving and healing many people during these rural mission trips. I saw the Lord break demonic oppression over entire villages and towns. We always told the people that it was Jesus Christ who had the power to heal and not men.

GOD'S POWER OVER THE WITCH DOCTOR

One of the most powerful moments was when we went on a missionary trip headed by Paul Busulwa to a rural village called Busembatya in eastern Uganda. We set up camp in a small mud house that the hosting pastor gave us and we began intercessory prayers for the village.

We asked Jesus Christ to save souls and bless the people with healings. The town was controlled by a witch doctor who forced most of the villagers to pay homage to him and to sacrifice animals to appease the gods. A number of people had died mysteriously at the water well. Our hosting pastor invited us to spend a week praying over the whole village and its well so that demonic strongholds would be broken and the people set free.

After fasting and praying for some time, we prayed over the well. We also prayed for healings, and God was faithful to answer our prayers. Weeks after we left, our host pastor told us how the witch doctor complained that his powers had gone and he could no longer do business. The witch doctor left the village, and as a result, there was a release of souls who gave their lives to Christ.

The harvest began. God broke the stronghold of demonic oppression over that village. Not only does God redeem men's' souls but He also blesses their villages.

During these numerous rural missions, God placed a desire for more of His presence, a desire to study His Word and a desire to be a blessing to the poor of the earth. We came to a revelation of Psalm 67:1 that God desired to be merciful to us, to bless us and to make His face shine upon us so that His name could be known among the nations. This is the whole purpose behind *The River Flows Down*. God's desire is that rivers of living water would flow through our lives carrying healing to the nations. The river Nile gives a very perfect portrayal of this principle. Millions depend on the Nile for survival, right from its source in Uganda to its end in Egypt.

KANSAS CITY HERE I COME

In March 1999, the Lord opened a door for me to come to study in the United States. I pledged to the Lord that I would give some of my time to go to Bible school. God opened a door at All Nations Training Center known then as Grace Training Center in Kansas City, Missouri. I was blessed to study God's Word and build relationships with Christians from other parts of the world. It was through relationship with other members of the body of Christ that I met John Gross and other wonderful Christians who have not ceased to be a blessing to my family and me.

During this time the Lord placed His burden upon my life and the lives of my new friends to reach out to the African nations of the Nile with the Gospel.

CHAPTER 3

Could I Be A Missionary?

It wasn't very long before something was stirring in the Charles' and I about going along with Kato when he returned home for a visit. This was especially challenging for me because my wife had developed a condition called Cushing's Syndrome. After many years of undiagnosed symptoms a specialist removed a small tumor from her pituitary gland. We thought she was all fixed.

After a year all Dianna's symptoms were returning and the tumor was back and growing. The surgeon said a second surgery would be dangerous because of all the scar tissue. I held onto the thought that God could just heal her. We drove to Canada and attended the Toronto Airport Vineyard to get prayer.

When we arrived the main seating area was packed and we had to sit in an overflow room. I heard a familiar voice, and turned to see a lady from Kansas City. She gave Dianna her seat in the main service area. There was a word of knowledge about Dianna and her disease. We both received prayer and were told that God had been using Dianna and her walk with God to draw compassion from His bride the Church.

The next thing that happened was harder to handle. One of the people praying asked me, "Would you allow Dianna to remain in

God's hand to serve out His purpose, knowing that the outcome will be a display of God's goodness?" With tears streaming down our faces we both said "yes," and kept on trusting God everyday despite the circumstances.

The medical expenses had all but drained us financially but without ever asking people to help, the Lord provided for us. Adrian, Missouri was our home and Victory Assembly of God was our church home but in reality God used the whole town to bless us. We received money in unmarked envelopes in the mail. Sometimes groceries would be left on our porch and we were even chosen to receive $800 from the Mayor's Christmas Tree Fund. Needless to say I could not argue with those words from Toronto because I was seeing it worked out on a daily basis.

Over the last 20 years Dianna has had multiple surgeries including three brain surgeries and one gamma knife. The gamma knife was the least painful for Dianna but the hardest to look at. It included a large steel helmet bolted into her skull, which allowed a very direct pinpointed flow of radiation to attack the tumor cells.

I want you to know that she never complained or became bitter toward God. She has more pure trust in God than anyone I have ever met. She depends on medicine to replace the natural functions of the pituitary gland. This is a constant reminder of how important even the smallest parts of the body are. How true that is in the church as well. We eventually moved to Kansas City, Missouri to be closer to Dianna's doctor.

THE TEAM'S PREPARATION FOR UGANDA

During our preparation time for our trip to accompany Kato, the Charles family and I attended a mission's class at Metro Christian Fellowship under the leadership of Floyd McClung, formerly of YWAM. This helped prepare us for the inevitable culture shock. We spent time in prayer and planning and endured the dreaded, though required shots.

I'll let Laura and Shawn share a little about their preparation. I want to emphasize again that these are just "everyday" people.

LAURA CHARLES

Traveling to Uganda, East Africa started as a whim. Our friend Kato was missing his family. As his spiritual family here in Kansas City, we wanted to send him home to visit. Well, John came to our home group the next week and said, "Hey, let's go with him!" This started our adventurous minds turning.

At first I thought, "How can we do this? We have a 12-year-old son. How could a mother in her right mind take her only child to such a dangerous place?" Trusting in God was not even a thought at this point. Did God really want us to do this? Eventually, I concluded that if God wanted us there, He would provide a way and He would be our protector.

SHAWN CHARLES

I work full-time as a street maintenance worker. Laura is my wife, a nurse, and Kyle is my son. Three years ago during home group we decided we would go to Uganda with our friend Kato. The only problem was the 8,140 miles between here and there.

You see I had never flown, and was not sure that I ever wanted to. After prayer, the Lord confirmed in my spirit that He would take care of my fears, and that this trip was part of His plans for our summer. We all came to similar conclusions and began to prepare for the journey to eastern Africa.

CHAPTER 4

Culture Shock

*J*ohn Gross: *In spite of good training in Kansas City, I was not prepared for what I saw that first day walking through Kampala as we headed for the Trumpet Center pastored by John Mulinde. The traffic was beyond description, with only one stoplight for a city of millions. Bikes, cars and trucks shared the bumper-to-bumper packed roads. I was amazed by the terrible road conditions. I am used to potholes but they have craters.*

We passed crippled people begging for food or money along the roads as well as well-dressed people on the way to work. As we arrived downtown I saw two little girls standing by themselves. They looked about five and eight-years-old. These were some of the orphaned, homeless children who sniff airplane fuel-soaked rags to keep emotionally numb and to cope with their dismal situation.

They were barefoot and their hair was terribly matted. The little girls' dresses were filthy. As we passed by they stared at us with their hands out. We had been told that giving them money would just further their drug problem, that giving them food was the thing to do. Unfortunately, I had no food so I reached into my pocket and pulled out two pieces of gum. I did not look at their hollow eyes directly, but as I handed them the gum, their facial expressions seemed to question, "What are we supposed to do with this?"

Feeling helpless I turned and continued my walk toward the church as tears ran down my face. I knew if Dianna had been well enough to travel she would be saying, "John, we can't leave them." I wondered, *What have I gotten myself into?* Later as the team reflected over the day I found I was not the only one feeling that way.

Shawn and Kato both preached at the Trumpet Center and encouraged the people that God was pleased with them and that they should not grow weary. I, however, was weary and continued that way all day.

When I fell into bed totally exhausted that night all I could see were those two little girls. I will never get over them. They are a permanent footprint in my heart, and will remain there as a reminder of Jesus' heart, "Suffer the little children to come unto me..." (Matt. 19:14).

I know they are on the equator and that food is plentiful. They will not starve or freeze to death. I know that we can't fix the whole world, but I was left grappling with the thoughts, *Where do I start and where do I stop? I needed the heartbeat of the Lord on this matter.*

VISIT, PREACH AND PRAY

Our new friend Derrick Kiboneka arranged for us to speak at several large churches including Kampala Pentecostal Church and we visited several of their small home groups. We felt very welcome at the home groups as we sipped on hot tea and ate biscuits (what we call cookies in the States). Of course I always had my eyes on the fruit especially the mangos and pineapple.

The home groups opened with a short Bible study then moved into a discussion of practical life application. It seems the Africans place a greater value on small groups than I have been accustomed to and that was encouraging for me.

We visited the Watoto Children's Home, known internationally for its choir. We didn't get to hear them sing but every church in Uganda has a choir that sounds great so I can only imagine how incredible they must sound.

We met with Intercessors for Uganda led by Laban Jjumba, who is known for helping unite Africa for prayer. He shared on the spiritual heartbeat of the nation of Uganda and its upcoming role in the harvest fields of Africa. He has eyewitness accounts of the east African revival and had seen great persecution there.

The East African Revival broke out in the 1930's and lasted for many years. It could be compared to the Great Awakening of the eastern United States under the leading of Jonathan Edwards. You would have a hard time finding many church's in all of east Africa that have not been effected by embers left by these revival fires. Even now the wind of the Spirit blows upon those embers.

We even got to share at a small Bible college that American missionary Tim Way helped start in a local Kampala Church. Shawn taught and I gave some practical life application as a follow up. Later all of us prayed for people in more of a one-on-one setting. Later we all prayed for a lady who had the rampant, deadly disease, AIDS.

AIDS EPIDEMIC

According to AVERT, an international AIDS charity, during the early 90's, HIV peaked at over 30% and until recently has been much higher than that in some areas. Uganda is now estimated by UNAIDS to have about 530,000 people living with HIV/AIDS. Uganda's Ministry of Health Surveillance Unit estimated that there were about 1,050,555 people living with HIV/AIDS by end of December 2001 and that there had been over 940,000 HIV/AIDS-related deaths since the onset of the epidemic in the country. According to the Population Reference Bureau the average life span for a male born in 1998 is 40 and 41 for a female. The good news is the numbers declined to 18% due largely to government programs teaching abstinence.

This precious lady invited us to her home and we met her young children who had already lost their father to AIDS. Though she was a Christian you could tell her heart was concerned for her children. What would happen to them after her death? This was truly an occasion where the words "I know what you are going through" seemed ludicrous. We had nothing to give her but our Hope. What a treasure hope is when you have lost yours. After we laid hands on her in prayer the look on her face seemed to speak to me, "It is well with my soul." I left with a greater resolve not to take my family for granted.

One year before, our friend Daniel Quinnelly interviewed the same lady in Uganda that was in the *Transformations Two* video (by George

Otis Jr. with the Sentinel Group). That testimony had encouraged me so much that I wanted desperately to interview one of the 200 plus people in Uganda who had been healed of full-blown AIDS.

Kato and I interviewed a lady named Margaret whose husband had died of AIDS, and who herself had been HIV positive. She had been totally healed and had the HIV tests and pictures to prove it. While doing the interview my faith went through the roof. This experience pushed me to start believing God for the miraculous and stop making excuses why God doesn't have to heal. Frankly I was tired of my excuses, Jesus paid a great price for our healing and I concluded the least I could do is believe.

DISTRIBUTING BIBLES

Metro Christian Fellowship had given us Bibles to share and we gave them to some Sudanese pastors and some rural Ugandan pastors from Masaka. Many pastors do not even own a Bible. They were overjoyed by the gift and expressed profound gratitude. They shared how they had been overlooked in years past as many supplies never reach deep in the bush.

One pastor had been walking many miles to another village to use a Bible to prepare his messages. Kato returned to Uganda after this first trip with more Bibles and told us about a children's church worker in Busia, in eastern Uganda, with a Sunday school for over 1,000 children. He had no Bible and told stories from memory. You can imagine his excitement when he received his own Bible.

As a man who has Bibles in every flavor, I was shocked. This burned in me up until my return mission trip two years later.

CHAPTER 5

Charles Family Testimonies

SHAWN CHARLES' TESTIMONY

I suffered culture shock for the first several days; I was stunned when we went to downtown Kampala. There were millions of people everywhere, walking on the sidewalks and spilling into the streets. The rest were crammed into early eighties style Toyota vans cruising streets that were in much need of repair. The sides of the streets were lined with little shops selling anything from used clothes to fresh fruit. When we went to some of the homes we had the opportunity to eat some good food, much of which we had never heard of, like *matokie*. It is made out of smashed up green bananas and served with many variations.

My heart broke over and over again, seeing all the little children that lived in the park. Many would follow us wanting money. I was very sad for all these children who seemed to have nowhere to go. I wept several evenings over their great need. The Lord was able to use theses times to deal with some issues of pride that I had been struggling with before we had left the United States.

The first time I preached I was nervous but each time I shared it was easier. I encouraged my newfound brothers and sisters in the

Lord. I let them know of the Father's great love for them, and pointed out the Scripture about not growing weary in well doing. I think the word was one I needed to hear as well because the Lord broke me before a room of 50 to 75 people. Thankfully Kato and John finished my first sermon when I was unable to continue.

God was faithful to speak to all of our hearts. Afterwards we met some of the pastors of Kampala Pentecostal Center and were blessed as they spoke prophetic words over our lives. Some wise, friendly and encouraging men and women of prayer are part of this fellowship.

The trip was great; all the trees, flowers and dark green countryside amazed me. Everywhere we went we found fresh fruit and friendly people. I loved going. I learned a lot about contentment from the people of Uganda and about the Lord's favor over them.

LAURA CHARLES' TESTIMONY

Because we were foreigners and white, we stuck out like sore thumbs. Everyone wanted to hear from the Americans. They really thought we had great things to say just because we were from America.

Another highlight was a surprise birthday party for me during a service with the teenagers who had adopted me as "Mom." David, Eva and Edward gave little speeches about their time with me and even sang a special song.

I know that the Holy Spirit used us as His vessels, and we shared the love of Christ, but what I gained from the Ugandans was far greater. I went to Uganda to share Jesus with them, but in reality it was I who received.

My favorite experiences were the divine setups. We met the people staying in our building. Will was a young man from Canada, in Uganda to work in the hospital as a pre-med student. One night we were worshipping in the gathering room and Will came out to listen. The Holy Spirit was drawing him and touching him deep in his heart.

Ivan was a young man from Kampala staying with his sisters who worked there. They had no parents. Ivan was quite sad and depressed. We spent time with him in the gathering room. Ivan took Will to church with him. We were able to give Will and Ivan Bibles. Ivan is now studying in a Bible College. Praise the Lord!

In Africa people with AIDS are called "slims," because they are so thin. We visited with Joyce, a mother with AIDS. She was so gracious to us. We were able to pray with her and give her son a children's Bible.

Americans could learn a lot in Uganda about being people-oriented, as opposed to being task-oriented and driven by the clock. Ugandans put out their very best for visitors. Most of us keep the best for ourselves so nobody will take it.

Kampala Pentecostal Center (KPC) sent us their best when they assigned three young adults to spend two weeks showing us around and helping us to communicate. David, Eva, and Edward were members of the college group called "Invaders of the Darkness." These young adults gave up part of their summer to spend time with us. They were great! It was as if we had known one another for a long time. They were fun to be with and very open to us. They loved the Lord Jesus with all their heart, soul, mind and strength.

The heartbreaking part of this trip was seeing the people of all ages that lived on the streets. There were many cripples. I thought of the crippled man at the gate Beautiful in Acts 3:2. I had nothing to give them. I so wanted to reach out like Peter, touch them and rejoice in their healing.

There were so very many children. My heart was overwhelmed with grief and conviction. I talked to one young boy of about 10 years of age. He spends his days on the street. The people he lives with beat him. He had been sniffing a substance similar to kerosene. It was so strong that just the fumes from him made my lungs burn. He said he knew of Jesus.

There were two little girls that were so dirty they were gray from the dust. I could tell that their dresses were really pretty at one time. They had no shoes. They were playful, as if they had no idea that something was wrong. This was a strange experience for me. I was unable to look at their faces or to look in their eyes. It was as if I would be overwhelmed with too much pain and grief.

KYLE CHARLES' TESTIMONY

The main thing I learned from my trip to Uganda is that we

Americans are so privileged. We have everything that we need. I do not mean we have everything we want, just what we need. The majority of the people in Uganda are not as well off. Many live on the street, have no home and scavenge for food. That was the main thing that touched my heart. With what little they have they remained content. You could tell they had a hard life yet they had a lot of joy. In spite of all we have, many Americans are never satisfied.

We always want more and more. I just hope and pray that one day soon we would come to realize that we do not need everything in the world. Truly all we need is God. He will satisfy all of our needs.

CHAPTER 6

Wrapping Up The First Trip

Toward the end of the trip we even got in a little R & R at the Nile River. We loaded in a large canoe-like boat. It had an old motor that had a hard time starting but eventually we made it to the very source of the Nile. We also went through Jinja to see the great Bujagali falls on the Nile.

There was a man, who for just a few dollars, would jump in the river and go over the falls, holding on to a five-gallon plastic jug full of air for support. I thought of how many times I have had to hold on to Jesus with that kind of intensity just to survive the rough waters of life. Kyle, the Charles' young son, had a good time as well; it's not every day that he gets to play with monkeys.

DIVINE APPOINTMENT

Soon our time was up and as we prepared for the long return home we prayed that God would give us an incredible divine appointment and it happened.

When Kato and I boarded the plane in Brussels, we noticed our tickets were messed up and that there was an empty seat between us. We laughed thinking God would ambush the poor person who sat there. As it happened a man sat down between us and asked us where we had been traveling. We told him we had been on a mission's trip. He said, "I should have known. My wife is a strong Christian, and she has been praying for me for years. Just today as I left the house she said, 'I am going to pray that God Himself will set you down between two men of God on your flight to convince you to serve Him.'"

Over the next several hours as we talked, he confessed his sin and actually led himself to the Lord. Many around our seats watched intently. The great commission still stands. It only waits on our response.

The trip just ruined me from ever living a "normal" life. I found a thirst that cannot be quenched with lukewarm water. I would like to encourage you to consider how you can help fulfill the great commission, "Go ye therefore into all nations and preach the gospel to every living creature."

LAURA CHARLES' TESTIMONY

Upon returning to America, I readjusted to my comfortable life and daily routines. For quite some time my life seemed meaningless. All of these experiences will continue to be with me forever. I pray they continue to change my outlook on life.

Not everyone is meant to move overseas as a missionary, but we can be missionaries in our own towns. I would not trade my experience on the mission field for anything. However, the same need for evangelism is right here in the great USA. I know that it is only the grace of God that enables us to walk the paths we are on. My humble pray is that I would walk well.

PART II

CHAPTER 7

The Return To Africa

Two years had passed since I had left the passion of the African revival fires. I was bored and felt myself slipping back into lethargy. Thankfully, I led a group of men and we studied the book *Wild at Heart* by John Eldredge. After a year I felt a stirring in my heart to return to Africa.

I started making serious plans in January of 2003 for a mid-May departure. I humbled myself and felt the Lord speak that when we came this year we should move out of the big city and into the village and bush where there are fewer people but with greater needs. Taking Bibles would be the main focus of this second trip. I was so impacted to learn on the first trip that many pastors have no formal Bible training and worse yet, do not even own a Bible.

THE TEAM

The Lord gathered a great group of people to go on this trip to Uganda. It was amazing to see His divine orchestration as He touched people's hearts. Below are introductions to each of the team members. Please note that no one is a pastor. They range in age from 36 to retirement. Who says God can't use anyone who is willing?

CHARLES OLSON JR. TESTIMONY

I have a wonderful wife and two beautiful young children. I work at a pharmaceutical company in Kansas City, Missouri, and live a "normal" Christian life. I was saved and baptized with the Holy Spirit as a young boy, and have had a personal relationship with Jesus for as long as I can remember.

There have been times throughout my life when I felt very close to Jesus, and times when I felt cold and did not live the outward life that I knew I should. In my mid-twenties, God renewed my heart.

Over the past 10 years I've taught adult Sunday school and served as a lay preacher and elder in the churches we have attended. In 1999 I went on a 19-day mission's trip to Honduras to help repair homes and encourage believers after the devastation of Hurricane Mitch.

My training has come from passing and failing many trials, reading and studying my Bible, listening to the Holy Spirit and striving to cultivate a heart after God. I have no college degree or major accomplishments to hang on my wall of fame, only a desire to follow Jesus wherever He takes me. And He showed me that he wanted me to go to Entebbe, Uganda.

CHARLES OLSON SR. TESTIMONY

When my son told me he was planning to go to Uganda, Africa, on a mission's trip with his friend, John Gross, my first thoughts were for his safety and for the family he would be leaving behind. I was flooded with fatherly emotions. I didn't like his idea one bit. My son would be traveling more than 7,000 miles away amidst the terrorism happening around the world. I also wondered whether he was going for the right motives.

I quickly discouraged him, hoping that would be enough to give him second thoughts. However, my son gently encouraged me to pray about it and went on his way. By the next morning, after spending time with the Lord, I had to call my son and apologize for reacting so hastily. Not only had God confirmed to me that my son was supposed to go, but to my surprise He showed me that I would be going with him!

I am retired, in my sixties and had never been out of the United States. I had some anxiety about going to a foreign country, but most of my anxiety came from my health issues. I had spondylosis of the upper spine and had undergone intestinal surgery several years ago. Since the surgery I have endured an extreme case of irritable bowel syndrome.

Traveling short distances from home was difficult and sometimes embarrassing. The thought of a 26-hour plane ride seemed impossible. But, as a man who has learned over my many years that God will not call me to something without equipping me, I moved forward with my plans.

As I began raising support for my trip, there were many times when I questioned whether it would be better for me just to send money with my son to help buy Bibles or to pay for their expenses. The question kept coming to my mind, *What difference will it make if I go?* I knew that the cost of my plane ticket alone could purchase many Bibles for pastors in need. But through my struggle, the Lord kept nudging me to move forward, and assured me enough money would come for the Bibles.

CHAPTER 8

God Uses Ordinary People

John Gross: When I woke at 6:00 AM on May 16, 2003 and turned on the television, I saw that British Airways had canceled flights into Nairobi, Kenya, due to potential problems with al-Qaeda. Our flight was with KLM, which did not cancel. The news reports urged Americans not to travel to Kenya, and our route to Uganda had a flight change in Kenya. I called Charlie. We prayed and felt the Lord said to go.

Dianna also gave her blessing knowing I had walked away without a scratch from a 70-mph head-on-collision with a drunk driver six months earlier. She figured God wasn't through with me yet and the safest place in the entire world was in the center of His will. I called all my immediate family and said my good-byes not knowing if that would be the last time we would talk.

I don't want to over dramatize, but I do want to be honest, I was tense with emotion wanting to hold on to my life yet willing to give it up for Jesus if that was His plan. I have always had thoughts that I might die for the gospel some day. I was fighting back tears as we picked up our suitcases, literally, and our crosses, figuratively, and headed for the airport.

Charles Olson Jr. and Sr. and I waved goodbye to our families and made our way onto the plane. With the great adventure before us we left Kansas City and eventually arrived in Nairobi where we boarded our connecting flight. We waited just off the runway for quite some time. After awhile the pilot announced that two passengers were missing, but their luggage was on board. With reports of terrorists being seen in the area earlier, airline officials took no chances and removed the luggage.

It's an understatement to say that from that moment until we arrived on Ugandan soil our prayers were intense.

CHARLES SENIOR TESTIMONY:

God provided financially through donations from His people. We were able to purchase 210 Bibles and on May 16, 2003, we boarded a plane at Kansas City and headed on an unbelievable journey. Twenty-six hours is a long time on airplanes. I was glad when we touched down at the Entebbe airport.

God healed me of the irritable bowel syndrome the moment we touched African soil. To His glory I never had a problem the entire time we were there and haven't since. That was just the beginning of the many changes that would happen to me while in Uganda for the next eight days.

John Gross: We arrived safely and were taken to the Entebbe Flight Motel. Unlike our first stay in Kampala we had our own bathroom. This was a real blessing. It made us feel like we were in the Hilton. Small things we take for granted each day can seem like major issues when we don't have access to them.

We slept a couple of hours, had a bite to eat and went to separate churches to preach the Sunday morning services. The need was so great and we were so few that we did split up to do most of the church services.

PASTOR'S MEETING AT KAJJANSI

Kajjansi is a suburb of Kampala. It reminded us of an old western movie set with small shops built right up next to the road. Makeshift buildings with old fashioned saw mills and pedal-powered sewing machines took us back in time. Hand-made furniture completed the quaint picture. In the background baskets of fresh fruit sat on tables and meat hung above on hooks. No Wal-Marts here. As we passed by the shops there were many curious eyes looking our way.

It is here that Jimmy Kigwana pastors a growing church. His relationship with the other pastors in town opened doors for us. One of the pastors volunteered the use of his facility that even had electricity to power a small sound system.

Life looked to be simple here. The people were so warm and friendly. We felt so welcome and honored to be there. The crowd of pastors grew each day as word spread further out into the villages. Some walked, others took taxis. Some even rode bicycles to the meetings.

We organized each day similarly, beginning with about 45 minutes of worship. Then we taught for about an hour and took a break for a noon snack. We provided bread and hot tea to hold over those who traveled from the bush.

A different church choir sang a few songs in a mixture of English and Swahili as we ate each day. We enjoyed experiencing worship with such uninhibited and free expression of love and adoration for Jesus. After the choir finished we had another round of teaching. Kato had flown in the week before us to spend extra time with his family and he brought a contemporary Ugandan conclusion to the service. He knew their hearts and took the things we said and wrapped them around stories they were familiar with. They responded with great emotion.

The people responded to every message with their whole hearts as Kato directed the altar calls. Sometimes the Lord brought powerful repentance followed by a declaration of faith, and other times, there was a "Yes" to the Lord for His purposes.

PAUL BUSULWA, UGANDAN PASTORAL OVERSEER

We here in Uganda highly appreciate the ministry of our brothers from the U.S. The team began blessing people down here in May 2002. They first sent a few Bibles, which we gave to three pastors who were sharing one Bible among them, others borrowed a Bible when available and yet these men and women led churches. Some had been praying for two to five years for God to give them study Bibles.

We became sensitized to the urgent need, which God met through the team that came in 2003 in conjunction with the rest who contributed. We equipped three Bible colleges, each having 35-40 student pastors plus other pastors and ministers of the gospel down this way.

The need is still great because God is leading us into new areas to equip the body of Christ. Please thank our brothers in America for extending your ministry down this way. The team composed of John Gross, Charlie Jr., Charlie Sr. and Kato ministered and prayed for the people. Many were transformed, healed and blessed and are eagerly waiting for their return.

We bless the church.

Pastor Paul Busulwa was the one who had discipled Kato and fellow team member Jimmy Kigwana. While there we met many that Jimmy and Kato had previously discipled. These were now young leaders. We saw firsthand the power and fruitfulness of relationship-based evangelism. The torch had been passed through multiple generations that all continued in covenant relationship with one another.

This was exactly what I learned during the time I spent training in Kansas City. Floyd McClung stressed, "Everything must be done through relationships." That statement together with Pastor McClung's life experiences on the mission field was foundational to me. Relationships became our support on the trip, and were the basis of almost all the messages preached. Everything about this trip was relationship based--NO LONE RANGERS ALLOWED. It was nice to see this being played out in Africa with good results. How I long to see this in America also.

The crusade mentality can be lacking in long-term commitment. If people are not immediately followed up on and hooked up with a strong relationship-based church many times they just fall through the cracks. Life is tough and new converts need real people with real commitment to disciple them in order to mature.

Jesus called a group of people who were so committed to one another that they sold houses and land to help each other through hard times. If each Christian in the world won only one person to Christ and then discipled him, then each new believer in turn did the same thing, it would not take long for everyone in the whole world to hear the gospel.

THE ORPHANAGE ALTERNATIVE

We also worked with Pastor Richard Kaaya of Entebbe Tabernacle of Christ Church, who has provided the most awesome alternative to an orphanage. He has started a Christian school with a boarding house attached. Those who can pay do, but many homeless children have made their way to Richard. Experientially the word orphan is not in Richard's vocabulary. This fosters an atmosphere of love and acceptance that is so needed in the western world.

RICHARD KAAYA TESTIMONY

I was born in 1960 and remained in Uganda during the Idi Amin era. I was born again in 1981 and after one year I felt the calling of God to ministry. Four years later I joined the Assemblies of God theological college in Nairobi, Kenya and received a B.A. in theology. I came back to Uganda in 1988 for pastoral ministry. In 1991 I married my wife, Debra, who was also from Uganda. In 1993 we pioneered a church in Entebbe. We were challenged by the great need of the poor and underprivileged children. Many of the children were not in school because their parents had died from AIDS or from the war.

Debra had worked with an orphanage and had also toured with the African Children's Choir, which gave her wisdom and insight for what was ahead of us. We did not start a traditional orphanage; we started the African Children's Sponsorship program. We raise support at $22 a month per child, which provides education, food, medication and living facilities.

The program is similar to an English style boarding school so orphaned children are living together with children who are simply boarding at school. When school is not in session the children stay with extended family or one of our church families. Debra and I have five children of our own and twelve more that we have adopted as our own.

CAROL BABIRYE: TESTIMONY (AGE 13)

I was born with a twin brother Joseph Kato. At six years of age our father died. Our mother had separated and disappeared a year before. We had no relatives living to take care of us. The villagers took us to the chief to decide our fate. No member of the village wanted us. The villagers abandoned my brother and I. We were left to fend for ourselves, with no hope.

Pastor Richard Kaaya heard about us and came to meet with the chief of the village to ask for favor. He asked if He could take Joseph and me to his home. The chief agreed and allowed us to go. From that moment on my fate changed for the better. I remained at Pastor Kaaya's home and another member of the church took in my brother. In 1998 my brother and I were sponsored by the African Children's Sponsorship program. Now we are attending New Life Primary School, which is a Christian school. This program has given me hope through Jesus Christ.

FURTHER INTO THE BUSH

We felt from the beginning that we wanted to venture as far as possible from the city to the places of greatest need, and that happened in Busia. Pastor Jackson Wadanya, who was born and raised there, had moved away to get a good education. He now works for the Ugandan Government, but he is different than most, as he has returned home to bless his people. He did not forget the place of small beginnings and returned to build a church deep in the bush. Mandre Eri pastors the church. He walks to visit his parishioners within a 35-mile radius. He appears to be in his fifties and does a great job of caring for the sheep of the Lord's pasture with the strength of a 21-year-old.

While there we saw 1,200 children packed in a church that might hold 300 comfortably in the States. After the children's service, 800 adults came in, also packed tightly.

We saw several healings but the one that gripped me the most was a middle-aged woman who told me, through an interpreter, that she had a tumor on her side caused from a witchcraft curse. I reached out and began to pray and break the curse in Jesus' name. The woman grabbed my hand and put it on a grapefruit sized tumor. It shrunk away to nothing under my hand. Honestly I almost fell over with shock as she confirmed her healing. It was her faith not mine, though mine was definitely stirred after that.

I started noticing many women with the same symptoms as they asked for prayer. I asked one of the interpreters about it and they whispered in my ear, "They are sick from being raped." These women were suffering from venereal diseases. What came to mind was the general devaluing of women that is intensified under Islamic influence. Remember, the Twin Towers bombers did so under the belief they would receive a reward of many virgins at their entry into heaven.

We are told that this religion is really peaceful and that the terrorists are just a fringe group. Tell that to the women of any third world country that live under its emotional imprisonment.

We prayed for the sick for a long time and never saw the end of the line that stretched out the church door. This place was so far removed from doctors' care that people suffered terribly. We held newborn babies burning with fever. We prayed for older ladies who were bent over and could hardly walk. We finally prayed a blanket prayer over them all because it was time to leave.

EVERYONE CAN CONTRIBUTE

One more thing about the sick. It is so sad that little children were so sick from drinking water that is unclean. Digging a well goes a long way, as does simple education about hygiene. I say that because there is a need for more than just preachers on the mission field. Simple teaching about hygiene can be life saving. Talents or knowledge you take for granted hold great value in the third world. If you have some talents buried, it's time to dig them up!

I have been asked by several Ugandan pastors to bring people from the States to help train the locals in industrial trade and farming skills. In addition there is a real need to invest time and money to help them start small business. Even teaching about sanitary food preparation can make a big difference. I see such wisdom in many of these pastors who just lack the resources but have the heart to help bring their nation out of poverty. Do not underestimate what God could do with just a few loaves and fishes.

In the evenings we all split up. Both Charles' with translators went to churches in Entebbe. I taught at a small Bible College in Entebbe where Paul is a regular teacher. All the students could speak

English, which allowed for a lot more freedom than speaking with a translator.

CHARLES OLSON JR. TESTIMONY

We had worked for months preparing for this eight-day trip. We knew that we were going to speak at a pastors' conference throughout the week, and distribute Bibles to them. However, when we arrived late that Saturday night, our friends in Entebbe told us that we had each been scheduled to preach in a church the following morning.

There I was a 36 year-old man, standing before a thousand African believers, waiting for the Lord to use me as His mouthpiece to speak His heart and message to this part of His body. I knew that I had nothing to offer these Saints, but I also knew that God was faithful. I believed that if I was willing to stand and submit myself to Him, the Holy Spirit would give me the Scriptures and words to say to encourage and build up these believers. The Lord did give me a word, which was well received. The Ugandan's enthusiasm made it very easy on beginning preachers.

Throughout the week, God showed us His faithfulness over and over again. As a team, we taught at the pastor's conference each day and then separated in the evenings to preach at various churches in Entebbe. God did not allow us to prepare much in advance—but daily He very sovereignly unfolded the overall theme of *The River Flows Down that became the title of this book.*

We handed out Bibles, saw many healed and saw many errors corrected by the Word of God. There had been a teaching going around that financial prosperity was proof of God's blessing. If a pastor did not own a car he was considered unanointed--even if he had miracles in his churches. Many who were poor lived under continual condemnation. We spent a long time talking about this misconception. These corrections set many believers free.

God used us to encourage many weary hearts, and to stir the Saints in Uganda to continue to fight the good fight, finish the race and keep the faith. It is an awesome feeling to be in a place where you know God has sent you, and to be giving the message that you know has come from God.

GENOCIDE IN SUDAN

John Gross: I met several students who were part of a community of about 200 Sudanese refugees. We invited them back to our motel to visit about future ministry together reaching into Sudan. They were working on translating the Bible into their own language. We presented them with eight study Bibles and a Strong's Concordance, together with a little money to help with their work. They were very touched that we sought them out with what to us seemed like small gifts. They likewise gave us a great gift--that of sharing many stories of their years in exile in both Kenya and Uganda. With that we felt so honored.

We videotaped an interview with them telling of terrible murders and mutilations within their borders. Several million people have been killed, yet it scarcely raises an eyebrow in the States. We listened as we were told how church services would be held under the cover of night. They dared not risk having a fire or lantern to give light for their service. That would signal machine gun rounds from a patrolling helicopter canvassing the southern regions of Sudan.

My eyes closed in shock as we heard stories of women having their breasts cut off simply to stop the life of the next generation. One of the men told about a recent trip back across the border. He did not recognize his own mother because she was just skin and bones. He could hardly get the words out as he told that even the local pastor was without clothes to wear. What a need for God's intervention! Let us be stirred to at least pray for them. How could we do less?

One Ugandan pastor said, "We were very reluctant to let another American in our village. The others looked like you but had a different message, one that caused much harm here. They came looking for us to sow into their ministry while you came sowing in ours. Thank you."

PASTOR JIMMY KIGWANA'S TESTIMONY

We are so thankful to our friends from America, who have done such a wonderful job extending to us such wonderful materials such as these Bibles and organizing the seminar. We really do appreciate and we extend our sincere appreciation to the home people who did a lot. They sacrificed whatever they had to see that these Bibles would come to us. We want to say thank you so much on behalf of Kajjansi New Life Bible College. We appreciate the Bibles, the Bible commentary and the Strong's Concordance.

We really just want to say THANK YOU SO MUCH and may God mightily bless you. And we conclude with this one more word. We are waiting for you to return next year. We pray that the home people will be supportive enough so that you may be available to us next time. God bless you so much.

UNTO THE LEAST OF THESE

John Gross: On Saturday, we were deep in the bush in Busia near Kenya when the sick began to come for prayer. There are no doctors or medical help there, so either God heals or death comes quickly knocking.

We wept as we prayed for hundreds. Many babies had unspeakable sicknesses. At that point, I knew for certain that when Jesus said, "Inasmuch as you have done it unto one of the least of these My brethren, you have done it unto Me" (Matt. 25:40) that I must always be a Mary, wasting myself on Him and them. I must let that river flow down; leaving all desire for the spotlight that so many consider the anointing. God, help us all to catch this one.

My father, a retired pastor, and my mother always had a heart for missions. God never opened the door for them, so there is desire within me to be a Solomon to their role as David so I can see the completion of what my parents only dreamed of.

WRAPPING IT UP

We had a wonderful traditional Ugandan meal with Kato's wife Jacinta and her parents and relatives. The main dish was a chicken steamed in banana leaves. As family tradition dictates, it was unwrapped, the gizzard was taken out and given to Kato to eat.

A side course was a large fish with the head intact, surrounded by vegetables served over rice. It was all very good.

In the rural Ugandan culture, the men eat at the table and the women eat together sitting on beautiful mats that are made of woven banana leaves. This is very hard to get used to but one must keep in mind we are not there to change culture but share Jesus. Jesus can change things that truly need changing as He transforms a nation.

This trip didn't allow for the day of R & R like the first trip, but we did get the surprise birthday party. Charlie Jr. had a birthday while we were there that was very special, not unlike Laura's on the first trip. Charles Sr. and I sipped our morning coffee slowly and stalled for time keeping Charles Jr. busy in conversation. The timing was perfect as Kato and His wife Jacinta came in carrying Charles' birthday cake. He enjoyed hearing his new-found Ugandan family sing *Happy Birthday* while knowing his wife and kids were home thinking of him as well.

An added blessing was a divine appointment with Parthy Evans and Alison Barfoot. They were also in Uganda from the Kansas City area on a similar mission with Christ Church, an Episcopal church in Overland Park, Kansas. We connected again when we all got home and had a great time comparing stories.

Alison has an interesting history working in Northern Uganda where rebel soldiers still wreak havoc. She has been bringing teams to Uganda to train leaders. She has been to areas where the conditions are very hard and has earned the respect of her peers. God uses ordinary people.

CHAPTER 9

Return Testimonies

CHARLES SENIOR

God answered my haunting question, "What difference will it make if I go?" in wonderful ways. As our team began teaching at the pastor's conference and various churches in the city we found that there was an overwhelming desire from the people for me to pray a blessing over them.

They all called me "Papa" and treated me with great respect. Being a grandfather of five and great-grandfather of one, I am respected in my own family, but this was far beyond what I felt deserving of. I came to understand the great absence of people, especially men, from my generation in the country of Uganda because of the great atrocities carried out during the reign of Idi Amin.

This mass murderer was responsible for 500,000 Ugandan deaths, 300,000 of which were Christians. His reign of terror in the 1970's included indescribable murders in the Nakasero State Research center as well as whole congregations, massacred as they worshipped the Lord. Many pastors and church leaders were killed leaving a huge void of older Christian leaders serving the Lord today. I felt in some way the Lord was allowing me to stand in the gap for those missing ones.

I laid hands on many people who were hungry for me to simply pray a father's blessing over them. The joy I experienced as God used me to bless these beautiful people was beyond description. Many people were saved, healed and delivered. Many lives were changed forever, especially mine.

Do not allow anyone or anything to discourage you from doing what God has put in your heart, because God sees from a heavenly perspective. You have no comprehension of how your words and deeds will affect God's people and their future generations to come.

CHARLES OLSON JR.

I was in Uganda because God had showed me His heart for the continent of Africa. He showed me the constant crying out to Him that comes from this poverty and disease-stricken place. It is so easy to turn our heads away from a place so far away.

Many times during the week I was reminded of my simple manner of speech and of my inability to memorize Scripture the way I would like. Yet, just as many times I experienced the joy of being used by God to meet the needs of His children because I was willing to go and simply submit myself to Him and to His service.

Let me encourage you, if you are open to missions, whether it is a one-time trip or full-time ministry, you will wonder how God could possibly use you. I say, don't be afraid. Pray and ask God to speak through you as His mouthpiece. He even spoke through a donkey once so He will not fail you, just as He did not fail me. We cannot let lack of education, lack of intellect, lack of speech abilities or talents to keep us from going where God wants us to go.

It is not about our abilities anyway. It is about allowing the Holy Spirit to speak through us and into the spirits of the people listening at that moment in time. It is about allowing the Holy Spirit to prompt us when it is the right time to give a hug or say a prayer or feed a hungry child. It is about being willing to be a person after God's own heart. If we do that, He will be faithful to show us His heart.

We respond by faithfully acting on what He shows us. He just might show us our purpose for being put here on this earth, as He did for me during my trip to Uganda, Africa. I learned to share the love of Christ wherever He opens the door. If only one person is saved or healed or delivered or encouraged, it is worth it all. Wasn't it worth it all to Jesus?

KATO

God has currently opened the doors to reach out with the Gospel to Uganda. Africa is experiencing a great prayer revival combined with a great harvest. However, there is a very large need to equip the saints in God's Word and balanced theology. This was one of our missions. I was so overcome with joy to be one of the instruments to be used of God to accomplish this.

I believe that Isaiah 18 spoke of Egypt, Sudan, Ethiopia, Eritrea, Kenya, Tanzania, Uganda and Somalia, as being involved in the end time harvest. God has a plan to use these Nile basin nations to reach out to the Moslem nations with the gospel of Jesus and also to be a blessing to Israel. The training that we sow into Uganda now will reap a mighty Moslem harvest in the future. A later chapter, *The Next Wall to Fall,* will give much more detail on this.

I remain grateful to the Body of Christ in Kansas City for participating in what God is doing in Africa. God has continued to bless us by opening doors to reach out to the Nile basin with the gospel.

Uganda is blessed that the River of Life family in relationship with other members of the body of Christ has allowed the rivers to flow to the nations of the Nile basin and the world.

CHAPTER 10

The River Flows Down

I want to let you know up front that I am passionate about this message for which this book is named. On May 20, 2003, during Kato's sermon I looked at the wall behind the pulpit. It had a beautiful painting of the Nile River flowing down over the land. The Lord began to deal with me. In my heart I kept hearing the phrase, *The River Flows Down*.

I was thinking of the first African trip when we had taken the canoe up the Nile River to its source in Lake Victoria, then took a van down to the Bujagali Falls. What a powerful display of gushing, rushing water spilling over the rocks. I just kept thinking that a river naturally flows down hill and if for some reason it ever flowed uphill how destructive it would be. If it overpowered its banks it would cause a massive, destructive flood until an obstruction eventually dammed it up.

Have we in more privileged countries been guilty of damming up the river of God? That is the exact question I wrestled with all evening. We have our denominational obstructions, we have our race obstructions, we have our gender obstructions, but most of all it is our pride that holds God back. The Lord is bringing a shaking and no obstruction will be able to stand against Him.

PUBLISHERS COMMENTS

As I read John's perceptions in this chapter it remined me of an open vision that I had on July 2, 1995 during my prayer time. I experienced an open vision of an enormous damn about ready to break. I could see the massive wall cracks and knew it would release menacing rapid water overflowing the banks.

Wading in the river were Christians on top of their belongings; (couches, computers, cars, etc.) as if gearing up to ride the rapids. Still others were holding on to their possessions as if the damn was long from breaking.

Then the damn broke! Water barreled down at full force. Those whose hearts had no attachment to their possessions were flying down upon them on top of the swift water as though the ride had been long prepared for. They were straddling all kinds of personal items imaginable, free from the cares of this world, the deceitfulness of riches and the lust of worldly things.

Yet the rapid water was overtaking those Christians holding on to their things which anchored them down. The screams for help as they twisted and turned from the strength of the water's power were piercing to the ears as well as the heart. Saints were holding onto computers and boxes of clothes. Some were attached to other people being tossed around and around and around. What a grievous experience to witness.

The individuals riding by swiftly had mixed emotions of exuberant joy and grief. It was excessively tumultuous with speed too great to attempt any rescue of those seized by the rivers' force. If they tried they would be consumed in trying. It occurred to me this vision was likened to the days of Noah and no doubt a warning to Christian believers of days fast approaching us.

Unmistakably this vision was connected to the great end time awakening implemented by the Captain of the Hosts Himself. The day to come is both a great day and a terrible day for sure. A day to prepare for by allowing the Holy Spirit to purge us of the lust and love of the things of this world and awaken us to the deception of our own hearts. May we fix our eyes on only one love, King Jesus our Lord.

— *Rose Rizzi Andrews July 2, 1995*

When we got back to our room that night the Lord began to unfold the following message that the whole team preached the next day. Charles Sr. prayed a blessing over the people and Charles Jr. and I preached the message tag team style. Kato came up at the end and called for the people to respond by saying yes to the River. We were all touched by the Lord's presence during the altar call:

Behold, how good and how pleasant it is For brethren to dwell together in unity. It is like the precious oil upon the head, Running down on the beard, the beard of Aaron, running down on the edge of his garments. It is like the dew of Hermon, Descending upon the mountains of Zion; For there the Lord commanded the blessing--Life forevermore (Psalm 133:1-3).

David is drawing a connection between the brethren dwelling together in unity and the way the anointing oil (symbolic of the Holy Spirit) flowed down on Aaron. I think sometimes we take the third person of the Godhead for granted, just like we take for granted how precious it is when brothers dwell together in unity.

The outgrowth of the early Jerusalem church in Acts hinged on the Church first waiting in one accord to be endued with the Holy Spirit's power. That power started with tongues of fire on their heads then went to their tongues as they spoke the Word with boldness. Finally it hit their feet and they became evangelists, running with the gospel, taking it to the ends of the earth. The anointing starts at the top and flows down.

How many of us get this turned around or maybe even turned upside down? We look at significant ministries and think, *I may be a nobody now but I'll keep walking in the anointing and one day it will be me at the top.* But God's ways are not our ways.

While in Africa I found that many in the western Church have presented Christianity as a pyramid, where the resources flow up to the top. In reality, the opposite is true. The resources should *always* flow down to the needy. I believe we are feeling the Lord's heart on the matter. He would prefer you to take the anointing He has given you and let it flow from you downward--to the poor, the broken, the lame, the orphan, the widow and the ones bound by Satan.

We might just as well quit trying to push the camel uphill through the eye of the needle. Let the spiritual gravity take the oil of God where it was intended to go—down, down, down. Joseph was thrown *down* in a pit, the three Hebrew children were thrown *down* in the fire and Jesus went *down* to the grave. Not bad company I would say.

I think we get the picture with the oil flowing down. Now, let's look at another symbol of the Holy Spirit, the river:

> *Then he brought me back to the door of the temple; and behold, water was issuing from below the threshold of the temple toward the east (for the temple faced east); and the water was flowing down from below the south end of the threshold of the temple, south of the altar (Ezekiel 47:1, RSV).*

I get excited reading these words, what a fountain remains to overflow to a lost and dying world.

> *Then he brought me out by way of the north gate, and led me round on the outside to the outer gate, that faces toward the east; and the water was coming out on the south side. Going on eastward with a line in his hand, the man measured a thousand cubits, and then led me through the water; and it was ankle-deep. Again he measured a thousand, and led me through the water; and it was knee-deep. Again he measured a thousand, and led me through the water; and it was up to the loins. Again he measured a thousand, and it was a river that I could not pass through, for the water had risen; it was deep enough to swim in, a river that could not be passed through. And he said to me, Son of man, have you seen this? Then he led me back along the bank of the river (Ezekiel 47:2-6, RSV).*

The River that is coming will intensify until only God can control it; only His banks can contain it:

> *As I went back, I saw upon the bank of the river very many trees on the one side and on the other. And he said to me, This water flows toward the eastern region and goes down into the Arabah; and when it enters the stagnant waters of the sea, the water will become fresh. And wherever the river goes every living creature which swarms will live, and there will be very many fish; for this water goes there, that the waters of the sea may become fresh; so everything will live where*

the river goes. Fishermen will stand beside the sea; from En-ge'di to En-eg'laim it will be a place for the spreading of nets; its fish will be of very many kinds, like the fish of the Great Sea. (Ezekiel 47:7-10, RSV).

Oh, let the fishermen gather. The harvest is plentiful. There will be no need to steal fish from another man's net:

But its swamps and marshes will not become fresh; they are to be left for salt. And on the banks, on both sides of the river, there will grow all kinds of trees for food. Their leaves will not wither nor their fruit fail, but they will bear fresh fruit every month, because the water for them flows from the sanctuary. Their fruit will be for food, and their leaves for healing (Ezekiel 47:11-12, RSV).

Here we see the future temple with a river running down, getting deeper and wider. We see the nations receiving healing from the trees planted by the river. The Lord wants the nations. He wants the river running down. I realize this is the millennial temple or God's kingdom on earth, so I do not want to take this out of context. However, Jesus did tell us to pray, "Thy Kingdom come, Thy will be done on earth as it is in heaven"(Luke 11:2) so I think I will stay with the thought on pretty safe ground.

Jesus is both the source of the river of life and the one who directs its flow. Jesus chooses to release the river from His temple the church, and only the church can restrict its flow. There is a great temptation to control the River of God. The issue of control flows out of fear. History gives us a glimpse of why this is so.

The church had removed itself from Jesus' control by the time of the Reformation. We find indulgences sold by the church with a promise of a quick exit from Hell, and even martyrdom for resisting church law. So as new and more appropriate reform came to the church, fear built new walls to protect those new reforms from slipping back into its dark past. However these walls separated the reform brought by men like Martin Luther from the next reform coming by men like John Wesley, which left us with so many options for the way we want to do church. Each option has its walls of protection but walls form a box and God can't be kept in a box.

This may come as a shock to us but the reform is not over. The box is coming down. We are still being changed from glory to glory into the very thing that Jesus waits for--His bride. Look closely and you will find reform within the mission of the church even as we speak. In the western world most of the flow of resources are used to run the local church. I would dare to say the river flows inward not outward. Many in the local church are beginning to find this abrasive and it is only a matter of time until the River of Life begins to flow outward again. The world is a dry parched ground crying out for water, how long will we cover our ears? Not long, for our hearts, though broken, are turned back to Jesus and His great commission. It is through our own broken lives that God longs to pour out His Love to others in need. His ways are matchless and powerful with such creativity that anything we come up with fails to compare.

What great and marvelous fellowship with Christ awaits us, as we allow Him the opportunity to release His River to all those who thirst for it. All we need to do is ask.

I have asked and have found that The River Flows Down. Ask and you too will see!

PART III

CHAPTER 11

Going Forward

My friend and pastor, Dave Christian, heard the Lord calling his name from Uganda. He and his pregnant wife, children and 73-year-old mother-in-law left the comforts of home and served the body of Christ in Uganda for a year.

DAVE CHRISTIAN

When my wife, Ruth, and I planted a church in Belton, Missouri called River of Life, John and Dianna Gross, whom we had met years earlier, showed up to help. That was our introduction to Uganda.

This adventure started on Father's Day 2003. I led the congregation in prayer for a young, fatherless boy in Uganda whom River of Life was sponsoring. I commented that Uganda could be thought of as a nation without fathers because of the death of a generation of men through tyrants and AIDS. The Ugandan church lacks developed leaders because of this. I had been fatherless growing up and am now a father. God showed me that He wanted us to have His heart and that we should be fathers to the fatherless.

After that service my boss at my full-time job called. (The church plant job was strictly volunteer). He explained that due to circumstances beyond his control he had to let me go. The nature of this event and my internal sense told me that God was in this and that I should not fight it.

I called John Gross but didn't tell him what had happened; I just asked him if he had heard anything from God. To my amazement he shared a remarkable vision that he had during the service that day.

In the vision Jesus handed me a piece of fruit. I was looking at the fruit as if to say, *What do you want me to do with this, eat it or give it to someone else to eat?* The Lord said I could eat the fruit and enjoy it, or I could drop it to the ground and let it die, then it would yield hundreds of thousands of pieces of fruit. After a long discussion about the vision, I told John about how the job had become a distraction to my ministry and I had been asking the Lord if it was time to let it go.

During three days of fasting and prayer, I heard the voice of God calling my family and me to a one-year project in Uganda. This calling connected with the vision God gave me years earlier to provide hands-on leadership development to a large network of congregations. I also believed that God was testing my heart and my faith.

I talked with Kato whom I met through John Gross. Kato confirmed the need and the invitation. If I didn't know Kato, it is very unlikely that I would have gone to Uganda--God works through relationships.

ALMA JONES TESTIMONY

I accepted Christ shortly after I turned 18. Almost immediately I knew that I would serve my Lord in Africa. I graduated from Northwestern Schools in Minneapolis at the age of 21 and immediately applied to various mission boards working in Africa. All turned me down for the same reason--I was a single woman under 25 years of age.

Angry with almost everyone–including God–I decided to show them. I would wait out the next four years and then they would have to take me. There is no place for anger in the life of God's children. It took years for the Lord to soften my heart to forgive. I married, had four children and lived a so-so Christian life, ministering whenever I had an opportunity.

My bitterness increased when I was forced to leave my children with babysitters while I worked various jobs. For His own purpose, the Lord opened a variety of doors for me to work as a secretary to the vice-president of a movie studio, the president of a large moving company, secretary in a one-girl law office, hearing assistant to an Administrative Law Judge and various other administrative positions.

All of the good jobs I held did not take the place of what I longed to do which was to be a stay-at-home mom. Since my first desire to serve on the mission field was closed for me; I decided I wanted to be "the woman behind the man in the pulpit." That didn't work out either.

The day came when God opened my ears to hear what He was saying to me, and I released all my anger and bitterness to Him. To describe what happened is difficult. It was like a large tree was uprooted in the very depths of my being. I was honestly free of my anger at God for not being able to serve Him in Africa. Repentance for this anger was exhausting. I wish I had listened to Him sooner. I wasted so many years.

More years passed as the Lord continued working in me, preparing me for a wonderful surprise. Now, at the age of 73, this great-grandmother is finally fulfilling the ministry God had for me all along. Our church has been asked to send a team to help a Ugandan pastor establish a resource center for the many pastors he has won to Christ and mentored. My son-in-law is uniquely qualified for this work and asked me to come along to be his secretary. What a privilege. I now understand why God put me in the jobs He did. I am staying in Uganda when my family leaves to come back home. I know this is God's second chance for me to fulfill the calling He has on my life.

I have been asked, "Aren't you afraid of being killed by the Muslims?" My answer is, "No!" As a child of God I know the enemy cannot kill me until God is ready for me to die. It doesn't matter where I am. When that time comes I will die. The choice is, do I die on the streets of Kansas City at the hands of a drug-crazed individual for no reason at all, or do I die at the hands of Muslims because I preach Jesus? It's a no-brainer.

INTERVIEW WITH DAVID CHRISTIAN

David is our firstborn. He is 9 years old, and was born in Kansas City. We talked with the kids and told them that we were willing to go anywhere and do anything that the Lord wants to do.

What do you think about going to Uganda?

"A lot of excitement. Most children in America my age probably wouldn't want to move to a place like Uganda. But I know that it's a place of the sun with the second largest lake and second largest river in the world. Some children may not want to stay for even a week but I'm going to stay for a year."

What is it going to be like?

"I'm not quite sure but I know it's going to be great. There will be some difficulties, such as the food. Every kind of food I will eat is going to be different than what I have here. I am going to try almost every food that there is on the Ugandan menu. I am practicing by trying new things right here in America.

"It's going to be a lot warmer than here. It won't snow but it will be nice and warm. And I don't know much more."

What do you know about the people?

"I don't know much about the people, but I can tell what most Ugandan men are going to be like from knowing Kato."

What are you going to be doing?

"Well, mainly I am going to teach kids who are about my age the Bible and stuff. I'm not quite sure what else, but I know I am going to do that."

What kinds of things do you think you'll learn there?

"I don't know what I will learn because I don't know what is there that is not here. Ugandan Biology: strange plants and animals."

Will you learn a lot?

"Oh yeah, I'll learn a lot."

Will we know anyone when we get there?

"No, but there is one person I 'know of.' That will be Kato's wife Jacinta. She will meet us at the airport."

Dad's Comments

David has raised money through a garage sale. He has given sacrificially from his personal savings, often putting his allowance into the "Uganda Bank." God has spoken to him many times regarding this project. He once had a vision where he was giving Bibles to people. He promptly went through the house and found all of his extra Bibles to give away. He really has a vision and feels a calling to go on this trip.

INTERVIEW WITH AARON CHRISTIAN

Aaron is my young son. He is 6 years old, and was born in Canada.

What do you plan to take with you?

"I am taking Gameboy, Froggie and Play Station."

What is Uganda going to look like?

"It's going to look like a small land. The people will be brown skinned."

What are you going to do?

"Teach the kids the Bible stuff. David will whisper in my ear and I'll tell them. I am going to help David."

Will there be children your age?

"Yes, maybe seven of them because I saw thousands of kids in the pictures."

What will you eat?

"Watermelons. Maybe porcupines."

Will you learn some new stuff while you are there?

"Yep, how to catch fruit from the trees."

What animals will you see?

"Lions, tigers, and bears, oh my, Snakes. Beavers. Swans."

Is there anything else you want to say?

"The End."

A BABY?

Ruth: As we planned to go to Uganda God made it clear to me that His ways are not our ways. Dave and I had left our family planning in God's hands, and I had not gotten pregnant in four years. Within two weeks of deciding to go to Uganda, Abagail was conceived. We had no insurance, no money and no idea what it would be like to have a baby in Uganda. From a human standpoint this was very bad timing. But God provided all that we needed stateside and the reassurance that there would be no problems with delivering our precious gift in Uganda. Because of my confidence in the Lord's timing I had no fear about having the baby in Uganda.

My first OB appointment was with a Nurse Practitioner who was interested in the fact that my husband was a pastor. That led into a discussion of our plans to go to Uganda. She told me that she and her husband have very good friends who live in Uganda. He works for the Ugandan government and his wife works at the United States Embassy. We were both amazed at the "coincidence" of our meeting. . On a subsequent visit she gave me their e-mail address and said that they would love to connect with us when we got there.

Six months before we got to Uganda Dave lost his job so we had to trust God for our finances before we left. Experiencing His provision opened up faith in our hearts for new possibilities. We raised support and Dave and I, my mother Alma, and the two boys headed for Entebbe, our home for the next eight months.

TOUCHING DOWN IN ENTEBBE

Dave: Even though we were jet lagging from about 20 hours of traveling I felt a great deal of anticipation wondering what God had in store for us as we arrived in Entebbe. It was 11:00 at night and too dark to see any of our surroundings. Jacinta, (Kato's wife) who was an airline employee, was there with about 15 people from the church to greet us—all carrying our luggage and hugging us. We weren't allowed to carry any of our bags, which we welcomed gladly!

The first thing we learned was that Ugandan people are remarkably hospitable and welcoming. It's one of the most noticeable things about their culture. At the airport they greeted us saying "You are welcome here." Richard Kaaya a local pastor was there. His wife, Deborah, took Alma's hand and walked with her. It took away any anxieties that Alma had and she and Deborah quickly became friends.

I've heard people say that Uganda is a great "starter" nation for new missionaries because the people are so friendly and helpful. I would agree with that statement 100 per cent. From the minute we stepped off the plane we were totally taken care of.

Ruth: The house we were supposed to stay in was being renovated but it wasn't done yet. Pastor Kaaya had connected with another Christian and arranged temporary housing that had miraculously just become available that day. The house had been a rental and was left in poor condition. Thirty people from the church worked all day to clean the inside, brought in bedding and converted a very uncomfortable, rundown house into something comfortable for us. They also cleaned the yard because there had been a cow residing there. When we arrived, people were still there cleaning so our welcoming committee was growing!

Generally there is no hot water in Ugandan homes. This house had a hot water heater but it hadn't been connected for some time. The owner was connecting it when we got there. Very few Ugandans use mosquito netting but they were very sensitive to our concerns about malaria and had the netting for all of us. They constantly inquired if we needed anything and wanted to ensure our comfort.

We had communicated with some missionaries from Oklahoma before we left. They weren't able to be there to meet us but had left a handcrafted basket full of bread and candy for a housewarming gift.

Within 30 minutes the lights went out. In Entebbe the electricity goes off for hours at a time. It kind of added to our sense of culture shock, but our new friends were prepared with candles for us. Two young ladies spent the night and for the first week someone was with us all the time. It was like having walking encyclopedias of the culture to interpret, help with language and explain about the foods and how to prepare them. (We cooked on a camp stove.) When we needed to buy a refrigerator or other things someone would always go with us.

Dave: We arrived late Friday night and Saturday Pastor Kaaya invited me to speak on Sunday. He is particularly gifted to work with long-term missionaries. He was very helpful to us.

I was still jet lagging but preached anyway. It was my first time to use an interpreter. I really enjoyed it because while the interpreter was speaking I had time to process my thoughts and listen to the Holy Spirit.

The interpreter had trouble with my Midwestern accent. Uganda was a British protectorate so they are more familiar with English spoken with a British accent and the British terminology. We looked like the British but we didn't talk like them.

My whole family had lived in Canada for three years while I went to seminary. The British influence in Canada helped us here. I began to adopt a more Ugandan style of English. God knows where He's sending you and will prepare you for your future sometimes without you even knowing it. When we were in Canada we never dreamed we'd end up in Uganda or that what we learned there about language and customs would be helpful.

My purpose in Uganda was to teach leadership training in the churches, to teach in a Bible college, and to minister in the churches as the Holy Spirit led. I preached revival services for six evening meetings. Some of our hosts were concerned that it might be too much but it was already planned so I plunged right in and it was great.

The meeting was outside Entebbe in a much smaller town/village. It was along the main highway and looked like a town but when we stepped behind the row of buildings there were thatched huts with no electricity and pit latrines. The farther off the road you travel the more primitive it becomes.

I preached in a church named "House of Prayer." The ceiling was thatched and the walls were bamboo tied together. They built the dirt up 5 inches higher for the platform. Attendance fluctuated up to 100. There was no electricity and no microphone.

The people sat on long, uncomfortable benches but for the

missionaries they had molded resin lawn chairs that were the seats of honor. Even deep in the villages they had them. The Ugandans show a great deal of honor to visitors and particularly for pastors and ministers. It was a little humbling for me to be on the receiving end of so much attention.

My mother-in-law, Alma, was given about 2-3 weeks before plunging in to speaking. She started by teaching 3-4 Sunday and Wednesday nights at one church. Then she was off to another location. She had never really done that before but they gave her quite a platform. Being a senior American coupled with her testimony of being called as a young woman and finally realizing her dream after all these years really ministered to the people. They respected and honored her and believed in her calling. The youth in particular embraced her. She'd get a few visits each week from high school girls.

She did well with the culture shock because there was always someone around to help and accompany her. She is more of a missionary by gifting. She learned more in a shorter time and got right into the language. I didn't feel that I had the time or energy to learn more than a few phrases but she plunged right in to learn the grammar. This is harder than it sounds because Ugandan is a spoken language, not a written language. She was able to find one textbook, which was published in the 1950's, to help western businessmen learn the language.

In the cities and towns the Ugandans are more likely to read English so we brought English Bibles to distribute. However, the further away you get from the city the fewer people read. English speaking pastors or translators are necessary.

Ruth: I was due in seven weeks so I set out to find a suitable place to deliver the baby. When I visited a hospital near Entebbe I was surprised at the low level of health care and cleanliness. Since we were in a city of 200,000 I expected more up to date medical facilities. I didn't want to have my baby there. Kato's wife, Jacinta and I went to Kampala, 30 minutes from where we lived, and I was encouraged because they had a more modern set up. Jacinta saw the delivery room and said, "I want to have my next baby here!"

My new Ugandan women friends were so helpful. When I went into labor Evelyn took us to the hospital and stayed by my side until,

Jacinta, relieved her. When it was time for the birth Jacinta helped with the translation. Even though the hospital staff spoke English there were still communication challenges. Some of their English was hard for us to understand as ours was for them.

Dave and Jacinta were interceding on both sides of the table, praying in tongues, and it was quite a spiritual experience. The birth wasn't any more painful than my others. The thing that was different was how fast my daughter moved through the birth canal. Abigail Ruth was born on March 9th 2004 at 4:09 pm. The doctor took her to clear her lungs and clean her up and Dave went over to watch. He told me later that he felt a spirit of fear summoning the spirit of death into the room. The doctor was having a hard time clearing her air passage and was becoming very fearful. Dave was praying and holding the oxygen to Abigail's nose so she could breathe, while the doctor worked for almost 10 minutes. I'm glad I wasn't aware of what was going on until it was over. It was the longest 10 minutes of Dave's life!

One of our friends said that witch doctors were very active in hospitals. Christian nurses and doctors constantly engage in spiritual warfare there. It's a culture of death, it seemed like our friends were always going to funerals--burying people from accidents, illness and AIDS. The death of newborns is fairly common.

After the birth I stayed in the hospital one night. We had asked for a private room and they didn't have one available. There were only two in the whole hospital. I was in a ward with three or four other patients who weren't all maternity patients. Curtains separated us all.

The hospitals don't provide meals. You have to have someone stay with you to bring your meals, give you your medicine, change your sheets and bathe you. You bring all these supplies with you when you come. The custom there is to eat supper at 10:00 at night. The lights were on in the ward; each of the patients had several family members there. They had their pots and pans and they ate and cleaned up and took a bath and it was about midnight before the lights were finally off. Then there was a late soccer game close by and after that a baby in the ward cried non-stop. We didn't get any sleep that night before leaving for home.

While in Uganda, we were able to get things we needed for Abbi like diapers and baby wipes. She got her immunizations at a clinic in

Entebbe that was very sanitary--compared to some others. I still didn't
have 100 % confidence so I prayed for the Lord to let the medicine
be pure and uncontaminated. The six months that Abigail spent in
Uganda were relatively uneventful. Dave was able to minister locally
and didn't spend any nights away for the first four to six weeks after
she was born.

Dave: The timing of the pregnancy was God's alone. Having a
baby in Uganda was challenging for us but opened more doors than
anything else. The greatest challenge that we faced was also the
greatest opportunity to open hearts. Since we came here while Ruth
was pregnant the Ugandan's knew we were serious and that God
must have truly called us. Abigail (which means "my father is joyful")
was a real crowd getter. Her birth forever connects us intimately
with this nation. She has a Ugandan name, "Namaganda" which
means "female Ugandan." When we introduced her by that name
the Ugandan's would always laugh, which was an expression of joy.
I wouldn't propose this as a missionary strategy, but whatever God
does to link you with the people be sure you don't miss it. He will do
something to connect you. We often say that Abigail is our primary
reward for obedience to God.

The Kajjansi area is where I did most of my ministry. It was close
enough to travel back home each night. For several months I preached
there every Sunday, plus conferences. The Bible college was also in this
area. Many churches participated in the Bible college and the pastors
got to know each other and there was great unity among them.

A high point of the trip was a time of ministry near Kajjansi. My
whole family came along. The Lord told me to speak to the children
and nine of them got saved. Then they asked me to minister to the
sick. Without prompting someone held Abigail so Ruth and the boys
ministered with me. Aaron had me pray for some sores in his mouth
and they were instantly healed.

It was wonderful to have my wife and sons with me as we laid
hands on the sick and prayed for healing. A young girl of about 13
was brought forward for healing and sat on a mat. I was proud to
see how earnestly my boys were praying for her. It was very special
to witness David's baptism in the Holy Spirit as he interceded! How
appropriate it was for God to pour out greater power when the need

was so large.

Healing is fairly common in the villages and many times the person healed doesn't even give a testimony. Their faith is very strong in the Lord. Most villagers can never afford to go to the doctor even though it is only about $5 US. What we would go to a doctor for they go to the Lord for. They need healing to be able to function.

Ruth: We took a five-hour ride to the village of Kamuli to do ministry. When we arrived, there was a small group of people but in just a few minutes there were dozens of adults and kids. They were shy and didn't try to talk to us very much but talked about us to each other. Even in Entebbe we were enough of a novelty to be the center of attention, in the village it was more so. Many people had never seen a white baby that young. Everyone wanted to touch her.

We went to a pastor's home outside the village. He had built a brick house, which was very unusual for that area. Close to the house was a traditional round hut that his wife used for her kitchen. They had gardens and fruit trees. They also had very healthy looking cattle and chickens. The chickens we saw in the city didn't look very healthy.

We did an outdoor evangelistic meeting close to the pastor's house. At least a few hundred attended and 20 came forward for salvation. Several weeks later we returned to Kamuli with a team from Kansas City. At that time we had a separate women's ministry meeting where several team members spoke and we answered questions.

Dave: Our first night there in our rudimentary "hotel" it was so hot that we left a fan blowing on the boys. Aaron woke up at 3:00 am with the croup. He had a barking cough and had trouble breathing. He was very panicked and so was I. I immediately thought about how far away we were from medical help. I couldn't call 911. It was only the Lord who could help. I took Aaron outside and the night was cooler than usual. This helped open his airway. If it had not been cool I don't know what we would have done.

The symptoms were gone the next morning but we learned where the closest clinic was and had Aaron tested for malaria, which was negative. We felt this was a direct spiritual attack because we were preaching a crusade, one of the first in the area.

Let me tell you a little about daily life in Uganda. My primary mode of transportation was a "taxi," which was a Toyota minivan, which can be seen in the thousands throughout Uganda. The public transportation system is very effective. You can travel anywhere within the country. It's very affordable and goes everywhere so it wasn't necessary to have a vehicle. A pastor did loan me a car, which was helpful when the family all traveled together.

There is no public school system and the expense is based on quality of education and facilities. Believing God for next term's tuition was a very common prayer request. Parents pay one term at a time and the cost for the less expensive schools is about $25-30 US per semester. That could easily be a month's salary. From our observation, about 80% of kids in the city go through elementary school. High school attendance seems to drop to about 60%.

Dealing with the government agency was frustrating because everything is extremely slow. Even with one of the church members there to help, I'd go to the office and have to come back with a different paper or the office would be closed. A visit took a whole day and it sometimes took four days to complete a transaction. We had 25 people who we could call on for help and we needed them all. They took us by the hand and helped in so many ways.

Life there is very slow, for the most part I enjoyed adapting to it. It was frustrating though when people came two hours late to an appointment. Their typical phrase was, "I got caught up." This means they talked to people along the way. Also, if someone comes to visit it is considered rude to say, "Come back later, I have another appointment." They invite them in, feed them and stay until the guests are ready to go.

Dave: We stood out everywhere we went. It was impossible to sneak anywhere. Once we just wanted to slip unnoticed into the back of a huge outdoor service. We didn't want special treatment but the ushers spotted us and whisked us to the front row. I started to resist but realized that we wouldn't be honoring their culture. We were seated next to the Mayor.

After the worship the pastor invited our whole family on the platform and since it was Jacinta's church she introduced us. Then, one by one, he handed each of us the microphone. David, my 10-year-old spoke for about five minutes. He had the whole crowd of about

2,000 laughing! During worship there had been some energetic, enthusiastic dancers on the platform and David shared his concern that the platform was going to collapse.

A woman who was the head of a Catholic/Christian school invited David to come and address the school. He decided to teach on laziness and he told the story of "The Little Red Hen" and shared a scripture about slothfulness. He had to stand on a table so all 250 kids could see. His antics on this shaky table made them all laugh. He spoke through an interpreter because his voice wouldn't carry to all the students. (Children in town are better at English than the adults.) His talk was well received. I shared a follow up and nine kids raised their hands for salvation.

Aaron turned seven while in Uganda. We had a family party for him. There are so many social functions that just having some family time was special for us.

Aaron wasn't resistant about going to Uganda, but he wasn't really excited about it before we left. His favorite pastimes were playing with his baby sister, playing Gameboy, and chasing chickens. He got along with the adults and kids. He kind of became a comedian because his white skin drew a lot of attention from the children. Thirty children would gather around to look at him. He would make faces and run toward them and they all laughed. He loved entertaining the children.

Almost every service included dancing as an expression of worship and he really liked that. He feels called to perform. He learned a lot by watching and he dances around the house. He had a dream three years ago that he was dancing before the Chinese so he feels a call there.

I think the most challenging thing for me was the difficulty communicating. Several times I talked to people for long periods of time. They seemed pretty good with English. Then I'd realize that we weren't even talking about the same things. The same words had different meanings and the Ugandans are very polite so they nod and act as if they understand even when they don't. This was so frustrating. I'd say that 90% of the time I couldn't communicate effectively without an interpreter.

Almost all of the time I traveled with a good interpreter. I was so grateful that he could relay what was on my heart to the people. I learned to speak slowly and repeat my main points. From time to time I'd ask if the audience understood. I also learned to watch their body language for clues. I offered many prayers of thanksgiving for the good interpreters.

Another time I was in Kamuli without my family and I didn't have my normal interpreters. A spirit of poverty oppressed the whole village. The people felt insignificant, unimportant and like they were never going to amount to anything. By illustration I told about growing up in poverty—going without shoes and not having much food. I wanted them to know that God can change their circumstances. I could tell that they weren't getting it. I labored over the story several times and finally moved on, satisfied that they must have understood.

Two months later, to my horror, I found out that the interpreter didn't relate the time appropriately. No one understood that I was speaking of my childhood. They thought that I was currently destitute and that my children didn't have shoes or clothing. They assumed that the ministry coordinator was stealing from me. They rebuked our coordinator for taking advantage of us and were ready to slaughter their animals to give us food. That was very disheartening. We weren't scheduled to go back so I did my best to have my coordinator explain the situation. I was so discouraged after that I was ready to go home.

We were not funded by an organization we just raised our money from friends and family. Neither did we report to any western missions group. This meant that we worked directly and exclusively with Ugandan nationals. The first five months, other than seeing the missionaries from Oklahoma, we didn't see any Americans. Our mission's approach was to work directly with nationals. We were just completely engulfed in the people and the culture. We didn't realize that until we were at a 4th of July celebration sponsored by the American embassy and we saw about 200 Americans. We were just flabbergasted. We ate hamburgers and hotdogs! So good! Most Americans live in Kampala and are government employees or aid workers.

Although we were going to stay a year, we had a sense of completion and felt the anointing begin to lift after eight months. Our sense that it was time to leave was also confirmed by dreams and prophetic words. I was glad to be going home, we all became ready to go about the same time. By the end of the time I had the sense that God had brought me to Uganda to meet these children of His because he is so proud of them. It was exactly like a parent who was showing off his kids.

Dave: We knew from the beginning that Alma was going to stay so we had been processing that all along and the issue was resolved. Leaving her in Uganda wasn't emotional; we had a peace that this was right for her. We also had a strong sense that we are going back to Uganda. I think that we, or possibly just me, will be back before 2006 for a short-term trip.

Ruth: The Lord arranged a great situation for my mother, Alma. Jacinta's aunt owned a nice house that she wanted to rent. Jacinta is in charge of overseeing the house and is my mother's landlord. She's in a good neighborhood and Jacinta took her to meet all the neighbors. A pastor and his wife live down the street so she has good support.

People in Uganda are very hospitable; they love to visit. The most rewarding thing she does is ministering to people in her home. They visit her all the time and ask her questions. She's attending a church in Entebbe, teaching the youth and leading a ladies Bible study. Another church in Kampala is using her to teach Bible seminars. She is 74 and tells me, "I have never been happier before in my life." She wants to stay until she goes to be with the Lord. She'll stay a lot healthier there because she has to walk and access to junk food is limited. She has a purpose to fulfill so she's got a motivation to stay healthy and a reason to live.

Dave: This Ugandan experience impacted us by revealing a calling to the nations. I never had a sense of calling to missions before but now I feel we could go anywhere. Before the trip it didn't seem possible but now we aren't concerned about where God will send us. We have no fear or doubt about going anywhere He wants. Since our experience in Uganda we know that all things are possible with God.

MISSION: POSSIBLE

Encouragement For You To Go

John Gross: I have concluded that young and old alike have a place on the mission field. I hope that by reading these stories you can see how God can use anyone who is willing. Formal Bible education is not needed as long as you have a teachable spirit and are willing to follow instructions from whoever is in authority over you.

I hope that you have seen that you don't have to be a polished preacher of the gospel to contribute on the mission field. You can hug a child, say a prayer over someone who is discouraged and sick or pass out food to a hungry person or a Bible to someone who is spiritually hungry.

Of course there can be dangers; however most of these can be avoided when a mission trip occurs through loving relationships that have established trust with the local people. "God has not given us a spirit of fear, but of power and love and a sound mind" (2 Timothy 1:7). With that confidence we can rest in Him.

Go forward from here one step at a time and one day at a time as the Lord leads. If you are apprehensive, spend time in prayer asking the Lord to make you willing to fulfill the plans He has for you.

If you feel a fire kindling in you for missions start reading books of great missionaries past and present. Start praying for missionaries on the field today. Saturate yourself with anything to do with missions.

Remember that the Lord can use any willing vessel. He used the Christian's children and he used their grandmother! God is not limited, but we limit ourselves by failing to trust Him. Remember God is writing a story in each of us about the river of His love as it flows through us to others. Reach out and touch someone with His river today.

CHAPTER 12

The Next Wall To Fall

S ince the Lord opened my eyes to what He is doing in Africa, I
have learned that the Bible predicts an end-time harvest to the
Moslem nations and that the northeast African countries will
be intricately involved in this. I believe it is crucial that they receive
training now so they will be prepared for the future. This is what the
Lord has shown me about Africa, specifically Uganda:

Walls of resistance to the gospel of Jesus are over all the earth.
Sometimes these walls are very hard to bring down, however no wall
can stand before the Lord and His army.

Some thought the Berlin wall would never fall. Communist
dictators in China have resisted Christianity and have hid behind the
Great Wall. Many atrocities have taken place, but even these could not
keep out the gospel. An international mission's organization estimates
that as many as 10,000 Chinese accept Jesus each day.

Middle Eastern Islam and the teaching of the Koran is a wall that
now seems hopeless to the church. People over all the earth are praying
in faith for the light of the gospel to shine through and disperse the
darkness. Our prayers will prevail.

There is a Jihad, a holy war, but we do not wrestle against flesh and blood rather the demonic forces behind them. Only prayer and Christ-like action will win this war. This is a separate issue from governmental law and order that opposes evil in the earth which is clearly defined in Romans 13:1-7. This battle must be fought in the Spirit and not in the natural.

God made us for His glory and we are wired for spiritual warfare possessing mighty weapons for the pulling down of strongholds. Our war will be won on our knees. It is time that the church intercedes from a higher place tucked under the shadow of His wings.

We must love Jesus with fervent devotion. We need to have an, "I'll do what You want me to do and go where You want me to go," attitude. Then as the Lord gives strategy and vision, arise with the same zeal that burned within Jesus to be about the Father's business.

The Father's business is the things He writes on our hearts. They are places and people groups that you have thought about--from your neighbor to the very ends of the earth. Begin to pray that the Lord would raise up laborers for the harvest fields. Are you available?

BEGIN TO PRAY

If you have never felt stirred for a particular place or people group, let me offer a way to get started. Maybe a friend has a vision to do something great for God. Why not make it a prayer project? You might be surprised what happens when you begin to show interest and join in prayer.

Join with me to pray for the fulfillment of the following verses from Isaiah and Zephaniah? God has a plan that's about to unfold for this geographic area known as the Nile basin in northeast Africa. Also called the Land of Cush, this area was far bigger in Bible times than the current Ethiopia. The nations represented by these verses could include Sudan, Egypt, Libya, Uganda, Kenya, Ethiopia, Somalia, and Eritrea. Christians from these nations will follow the old trade routes back to Jerusalem and bring the gospel to the Jews! The prophet Isaiah shared the plan many years ago:

> *Ah, land of whirring wings which is beyond the rivers of Ethiopia;*
> *which sends ambassadors by the Nile, in vessels of papyrus on the*

waters! Go, you swift messengers, to a nation, tall and smooth, to a people feared near and far, a nation mighty and conquering, whose land the rivers divide. All you inhabitants of the world, you who dwell on the earth, when a signal is raised on the mountains, look! When a trumpet is blown, hear! For thus the Lord said to me: "I will quietly look from my dwelling like clear heat in sunshine, like a cloud of dew in the heat of harvest." For before the harvest, when the blossom is over, and the flower becomes a ripening grape, he will cut off the shoots with pruning hooks, and the spreading branches he will hew away. They shall all of them be left to the birds of prey of the mountains and to the beasts of the earth. And the birds of prey will summer upon them, and all the beast of the earth will winter upon them. At that time gifts will be brought to the Lord of hosts from a people tall and smooth, from a people feared near and far, a nation mighty and conquering, whose land the rivers divide, to Mount Zion, the place of the name of the Lord of hosts (Isaiah 18:1-7, RSV)

The Prophet Zephaniah offers further insight into the role of Africa: "From beyond the rivers of Ethiopia My worshipers, My dispersed ones, Will bring My offerings" (Zephaniah 3:10).

Let's look at the rivers of Ethiopia in several reference materials. The *Wycliffe Bible Commentary* (Moody Press, 1962) says about Isaiah 18:7, "Here the Ethiopians are identified as coming from the land where the Blue Nile joins the White Nile."

The *Zondervan Compact Bible Dictionary* (1981) further explains about the Ethiopia of Isaiah 18, "Ethiopia was a sparsely populated land traversed by the Blue and the White Nile and their tributaries, a reservoir of hardy manpower for ambitious rulers."

Some might find a little difference in the definition, but researchers speak of the land divided by the two Niles. The Blue Nile and the White Nile converge, flowing into one river, the Nile River.

These nations have suffered greatly from famine, war and disease. Millions of Christians have died in some of these nations. The term "seed of the martyrs" has been proven true many times over. God brings a harvest of souls from the lands where people died for their faith. For this reason alone we should have great faith for revival there.

The gift or blessings referred to in Isaiah 18:7 and Zephaniah 3:10 is none other than the good news of Jesus being taken to Mount Zion. I, along with many others, believe that African evangelists will preach the gospel all the way back to Jerusalem.

While we were in Uganda we heard many Christians talking about Isaiah 18. They sincerely believe their destiny is forever linked to its fulfillment. Sometime later I had the privilege of being on a prayer team traveling throughout Israel Egypt and Ethiopia. While we were in Ethiopia I asked several Church leaders their opinion of Isaiah's prophecy. They shared the same view I had found in Uganda.

Just as the ancient trade routes delivered goods to Jerusalem, the good fruit of the gospel will find its way back home to the place it all started--Jerusalem. If you hold to the view that God is done with natural Israel, I ask you from the bottom of my heart, please hear me out.

Transition with me to the nation of Israel and I will tie these two regions together. God loves natural Israel. According to the book of Romans He has one last big surprise for them, "open eyes." I recently read the book *Can These Bones Live?* This eyewitness account of spiritual renewal in Israel, written by missionary Chandler Lanier, has stirred my faith.

Jewish eyes are opening to find Jesus as their Messiah. While not yet happening in overwhelming numbers, growth continues. If the Gentile church would begin to cry out for Jewish salvation with the same intensity that anti-Semitic men have sought Israel's destruction, what might God do?

Read on and let God's words speak to you: "I say then, has God cast away His people? Certainly not! For I also am an Israelite, of the seed of Abraham, of the tribe of Benjamin. God has not cast away His people whom He foreknew" (Romans 11:1-2, NKJ).

It is very clear throughout scripture that God has not finished with natural Israel.

It is the same today, for not all the Jews have turned away from God. A few Jews are being saved as a result of God's kindness in choosing them. And if they are saved by God's kindness, then it is not by their good works. For in that case, God's wonderful kindness would not be what it really is—free and undeserved. So this is the situation: Most of the Jews have not found the favor of God they are looking for so earnestly. A few have—the ones God has chosen—but the rest were made unresponsive. As the Scriptures say, "God has put them into a deep sleep. To this very day he has shut their eyes so they do not see, and closed their ears so they do not hear." David spoke of this same thing when he said, "Let their bountiful table become a snare, a trap that makes them think all is well. Let their blessings cause them to stumble. Let their eyes go blind so they cannot see, and let their backs grow weaker and weaker." Did God's people stumble and fall beyond recovery? Of course not! His purpose was to make his salvation available to the Gentiles, and then the Jews would be jealous and want it for themselves. Now if the Gentiles were enriched because the Jews turned down God's offer of salvation, think how much greater a blessing the world will share when the Jews finally accept it (Romans 11:5-12, TNLT).

God Himself blinded Israel's eyes so we Gentiles could be saved. This seems very clear from this passage: "Now if their fall is riches for the world, and their failure riches for the Gentiles, how much more their fullness" (Romans 11:12, NKJ)! When they see, what will be our fullness? "For if their being cast away is the reconciling of the world, what will their acceptance be but life from the dead" (Romans 11:15, NKJ)?

Life from the dead. Where have we read that before? Similar language is used when speaking of the resurrection in Romans 8:11.

For I do not desire, brethren, that you should be ignorant of this mystery, lest you should be wise in your own opinion, that hardening in part has happened to Israel until the fullness of the Gentiles has come in. And so all Israel will be saved, as it is written: "The Deliverer will come out of Zion, And He will turn away ungodliness from Jacob; For this is My covenant with them, When I take away their sins." Concerning the gospel they are enemies for your sake, but concerning the election they are beloved for the sake of the fathers. For the gifts and the calling of God are irrevocable (Romans 11:25-29, NKJ).

Thank God His gifts and callings are irrevocable!

Oh, the depth of the riches both of the wisdom and knowledge of God! How unsearchable are His judgments and His ways past finding out! "For who has known the mind of the Lord? Or who has become His counselor?" "Or who has first given to Him And it shall be repaid to him?" For of Him and through Him and to Him are all things, to whom be glory forever. Amen (Romans 11:33-36, NKJ).

Let us add our Amen! God has a plan and it's a big one. Now let's return to the Ethiopia Scriptures. There is a recent connection with some of this land and natural Israel.

In 1973 Ethiopian Jews were known as Beta Israel or the House of Israel. In 1984, Israel led an airlift called Operation Moses and rescued almost 8,000 Jews who were starving in Sudanese refugee camps.

Operation Solomon brought most of the remaining Ethiopian Jews (about 14,000) to Israel in 1991. Of course many Jews have left Europe, Russia and Germany since the early 1900's too. What a blessing to the Lord for His children to return to their land.

This all started after almost 2,000 years of the Jews being dispersed to the nations. Theodor Herzl, the father of the Zionist movement, got the vision to return to the Promised Land in 1895.

There is another Israel connection, this time with Uganda. This idea was never implemented but Uganda was almost used as a temporary settlement for the Jews in the early 1900's. Anti-Semitic emotions were stirred all over Europe and in Russia great persecution was rising resulting in the death of many Jews. Herzl after approaching many leaders about the possibility of a Jewish state was offered 5,000 acres of land in Uganda by British Foreign Secretary Lord Lansdowne. The Russian Jews refused the offer believing any Zion without Jerusalem is no Zion at all. Because of this offer, Uganda would hold a special place in Israel's future. This gave new fuel for the fire of Zionism, which was ultimately realized in 1948, when Israel once again became a nation.

More Jews are residing in the area of Mount Elgon in eastern Uganda. They are known as the Abayudaya Jews of Uganda They have just recently been given attention by several Jewish affiliated agencies.

Also worth noting is the Entebbe Rescue Mission. It started on June

27, 1976, when terrorists from the Front for the Liberation of Palestine and their German accomplices controlling an Air France Airbus forced a landing at the Entebbe airport. On July 3, Israeli soldiers fought and freed the 105 Jewish hostages, killing the highjackers in less than an hour. Back in the USA on the 4th of July, news broadcasters told of one of the greatest rescue attempts of all time. Attacks of terrorism and great persecution will forever link Uganda and Israel.

Of course the greatest rescue of all times is the rescue provided through the cross of Jesus and His shed blood. He is still in the business of rescuing the perishing. All over the earth there is hatred for Jesus and His followers. I believe with all that is within me that Ugandan Christians are being prepared by the Lord. Because of their terrible history with persecution, God will use them as evangelists to move into Muslim-controlled nations. They need us to pray and help finance their call. Will we come alongside them and help?

The Nile starts at Lake Victoria in Uganda, and empties itself in the Mediterranean Sea, which also borders Israel. Here is the real road map for the peace that has eluded Israel. Pray that God would cause His River of Life to flow like the Nile northward from Uganda, Sudan, Kenya, Ethiopia, Somalia, Eritrea, Egypt, and Libya, even to Israel.

Sometimes Americans think we are God's chosen people, but God blesses America because we have blessed Israel. Up to this point, we have been the missionaries. I believe the mantle is about to change

The fastest growing denominations in the USA usually include the growth numbers from their African missionary endeavors. The African harvest is ready, but prepared laborers are in short supply. It's time we invested in the idea of indigenous missions—local people winning local people to Jesus.

Indigenous missions—remember those words and their meaning. God has not called us to make Americans, but disciples. The fields are white, so let's humble ourselves and raise up disciples to be leaders to reach their own people. Then love those disciples and help them the way they want to be helped to retain the harvest. The nets must be strong enough to hold the harvest. The indigenous people have suffered under the hands of evil men and know what it takes to walk the walk. They will head north into enemy territory. Many are dying there now. Let us stand with them.

AN EYE-WITNESS:

I thank God for my brother in Christ, John Gross. Here in Ethiopia it is amazing to watch God unfolding His original plan prophesied in Isaiah 18:1-7, (see page 78). It is just as John stated. Many Ethiopian Jews called, Beta Israel, return to their land!

My wife and I are from Gondor, Ethiopia. We know pastors serving the Lord in this difficult place. Thank God for willing messengers to preach the Good News in such darkness. As a result of these servants, my wife and I have given our lives to Jesus Christ. We too believe the Lord will send His mighty power and use us in His Kingdom work.

We will no longer be called Africa, meaning "the dark continent." I believe as the light of the Gospel continues to shine forth, we will forever be changed.

Fulfilling the Promise,
Rev. Gizaw D. Dersch
Ethiopian Evangelical Christian Association
Executive Director

> **Prayer:** Father, bless us with everything we need to finish the race set before us. I pray for the peace of Jerusalem; that you would remove the veil from their eyes, so that they might see Jesus, their Messiah, and that Israel would be saved. I pray that You would raise up the Ugandan people as missionaries, to make converts of the Arab Muslims who have persecuted them. I pray for the salvation of the Muslims all over the earth, but specifically in Sudan. Please bring a stop to the terrible violence there. Please move by you Holy Spirit and prepare us as the Bride for Your dear Son. We believe the walls will come down by Your mighty power... Use us.
>
> In Jesus Name I prayer Amen. – *John Gross*

THE POEM

While writing this book the Lord gave me this poem about the ultimate destination of the River that flows down.

The Source of the Nile

See these people who are Dark and Tall
They will not hide but boldly face the wall
The wall to the north has plans to move south
It can only be stopped with the sword in Christ's mouth
What suffering in Uganda and now in Sudan
From the terror of Islam with their sword in their hand
A great battle is raging while some sit in slumber
Jesus has come with an army none can number
Our Lord is standing and now leads our ways
Radiant beauty bursts forth; He's the Ancient of Days
His days have been planned from the beginning 'til now
When He appears in the clouds all the nations will bow
From Jerusalem to Judea the Gospel did go
To Samaria and places the Holy Spirit would show
Even to Gentiles the great seed of the gospel was sown
Now it's back to Jerusalem the winds of change have blown
Fiery evangelists from the source of the Nile
From their bellies flow God's river mile after mile
With Prayer at the border they move to Sudan
The wall of Islam is falling; they are off to the Promised Land

(There is a growing move in the world to take the gospel back to Jerusalem. I urge you to study this further. A great example of this is happening in China. You can read about it in the book *Back To Jerusalem* written by Paul Hattaway).

APPENDIX

LIFESTYLE ISSUES

LIFESTYLE ISSUES

Lifestyle issues are a major consideration in going from the comfort of western society into a third world country. One thing to consider is the issue of food and water. Be prepared. Drinking the water can make you very sick if it is not boiled. Where possible keep a supply of bottled water that have not had their seals broken.

One must be careful when consuming food, fresh fruit should always be washed with your own bottled water or water that has been boiled. Even in restaurants we avoided lettuce salad because the leaves were probably washed with tap water. Also, realize ice is a rare commodity so a cold drink is cool at best.

Beware of meats or cooked items that have been set out by street vendors. You don't know if the food was properly stored or prepared. The best thing is to always have a local person with you who is used to having westerners around to help watch out for trouble. While there are probably many things that you could eat and not get sick, it's always preferable to err on the side of caution.

When you are eating at someone's home you may be served something that you would rather not eat. As long as the food is safe, please be sensitive to the host's feelings, they could be very hurt if you refuse. Many times the host has made a significant financial sacrifice to purchase and prepare the very best food for you. I am a picky eater, and this was one of the hardest things for me.

I actually spent a lot of time asking the Lord to change my actions and feeling. He has brought me a long way. With faith I say don't allow something so petty to stand in the way of following God.

Study the culture of the area where you will be traveling. Remember what one thing means where you live may mean the opposite where you are going. Let me give you an example. I grew up in the country. There a man has a good firm handshake. If a man shakes hands softly, many secretly question his masculinity. In Uganda most men who have not been around Americans much have a soft handshake. When I eventually asked about the difference, I found that our cultures were almost opposite in viewpoint. I discovered that the way I was coming across could be seen as very rude. When in Rome, do as the Romans do.

Make sure you are current on your immunizations and that you take measures for protection from mosquitoes. Know the laws and customs of the area and ensure that the embassy or consulate of your country knows you are there. Take some basic medical supplies and someone who knows fundamental first aid. If that's not possible take a class yourself. It might come in handy. Travel in three's when possible, having a male in each group.

Most importantly put together a prayer team of people that have a personal history with you and who will honestly pray. *Don't leave home without it!*

Short-Term Missions Opportunities are Year Round

(A missions organization endorsed by the publisher)

We have ministry opportunities that span twelve months of the year. This enables your Short-Term Mission trip to fit your schedule and the type of team ministry you are prepared to do.

Types of ministry For Short-Term Mission Teams:

Children's Ministry:

Vacation Bible School Program from 3 - 5 days; using cassettes [in their language] of songs & puppet skits, clowns, crafts, drama and other creative forms of teaching. With the use of Interpreters or just God's love being shared, the warmth, responsiveness and beauty of the children will overwhelm your team.

Church Services:

On Sunday, as well as evening services during the week ... Your team can provide preaching, teaching, music, testimonies, creative arts, prayer ministry ... Your team will be enthusiastically received as they share God's love and encourage His people.

Street Evangelism:

The Harvest is truly ripe! The eagerness of multitudes to give their hearts to Jesus is almost staggering! Your team can serve Church leaders through presentation of the gospel with the use of Mime, Drama and Testimony; followed by your Host Church leader or a team member of his choice, preaching and giving invitation to receive Christ. As your team prays with those who respond there will often be dramatic encounters with the Living God! Your team can also use Flags, Banners and Dance in their presentations.

Village Ministry:

Your team may desire to travel into small rural villages. Where they can distribute clothing, minister in prayer, and share God's Love. Many of these remote villages are filled with abject poverty and the people receive very little help. Often the poverty is both of body and soul ... where the Love of God is so needed. If your team is ready to "rough it", a village trip of several days can be arranged.

Church Building:

You may desire to form or join a building team to plan and focus on construction work. It is a great blessing to a Host Church, and their pastor, to have help moving their building project forward. As your team builds they, themselves, will be built up!

Medical Teams:

We have been encouraged in seeing the lasting fruit of the ministry of medical teams. Our teams have ministered in cities and rural mountain villages. There is such a great need for medical care in many areas where it isn't available. By partnering with the national medical professionals, we are able to minister to the physical need of the people; as well as to their spiritual need. Many come to know the Lord Jesus as they are touched by His Love through Harvest Preparation medical teams.

Here's your opportunity to get started:

Contact:

neal@harvestpreparation.com
Harvest Preparation International Ministries
455 Interstate CT. Sarasota FL. 34240
941-330-9753

OTHER BOOKS AVAILABLE THROUGH
AMBASSADOR PRESS

816-965-0509 • fax 877-858-1932
www.ambassadors-international.com

Sounds of Heaven by Rose Rizzi Andrews
An eye opening account of music
in the Bible
ISBN 09675552-2-1

**Fire of God's Presence by
Owen Murphy & John Wesley Adams**
An account of the Hebrides Revival
ISBN 0-9675552-1-3

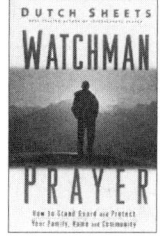

Feet to the Street by Rose Rizzi Andrews
A powerful picture of prophetic
prayer evangelism
ISBN 0-9675552-0-5

Prophetic Etiquette by Michael Sullivant
A "how to" book for prophecy
ISBN 0-9675552-2-1

Watchman Prayer by Dutch Sheets
How to stand guard and protect your
family, home and community
ISBN 0-83072568-7

Unrelenting Prayer by Bob Sorge
Eeceive a holy resolve to enter
into an abandoned lifestyle
ISBN 0-97496643-6

AMBASSADORS PRESS

A PUBLISHING MINISTRY FOR PROVEN FIVE FOLD MINISTERS

"Leaving behind a written legacy for the next generation."

ORDER FORM

(Suggested donation)

I would like to order:

- ☐ **The Fire of God's Presence,**
  Owen Murphy *& John Wesley Adams* . . . . $ 9.99
- ☐ **Sounds of Heaven,** *Rose Rizzi Andrews* 9.99
- ☐ **Prophetic Etiquette,** *Michael Sullivant* 12.99
- ☐ **Watchman Prayer,** *Dutch Sheets* 13.99
- ☐ **Unrelenting Prayer,** *Bob Sorge* 11.99
- ☐ **Feet to the Street,** *Rose Rizzi Andrews* 10.99

Total # of books_____ *(shipping & handling, add $3.25 ea.)*

Total amount enclosed $ _____

All proceeds are contributions to further our publishing ministry.

Name _____

Address _____

City _____State _____Zip _____

Phone (day) _____ Phone (evening) _____

Allow up to 4 weeks for delivery ($25.00 return check fee).
Please make Checks or Money Orders Payable to:
AMBASSADORS INTERNATIONAL